Fly Fishing
California
Stillwaters

THE BEST TROUT LAKES

THE BEST TROUT LAKES

Fly Fishing
California
Stillwaters

Bill Sunderland

Photographs by Rick E. Martin

MOSCA LOCA BOOKS, INC.

First Edition published in 2001 by:
    Mosca Loca Books, Inc.
    865 Beach Road
    Whitethorn, CA 95589
    (707) 986-1683
www.flyfishcaliforniabooks.com

Design and maps by David Frazier

Editing by Bud Bynack

Flies tied by Jeff Yamagata (Pages 24, 26, 27, 88, 92,
103, 112, 116, 121, 122, and 127) and Terry Edelmann
(Pages 22 and 75)

Fly fishing collectables courtesy of Dennis Buranek

With special thanks for sharing their knowledge to:
Peter Bauer, Frank Bertaina, Andy Burk, Richard Burns,
Jim Crouse, Terry Edelmann, Wayne Eng, Jay Fair,
Michael Fisher, Fred Gordon, Gary Gunsolley,
Del Heacock, Cal and Mike Kalpin, John King,
Terry Knight, Mike Kuczynski, Joe Neil, and Galen Petty.

ISBN: 0-9708576-3-2

Printed in Singapore

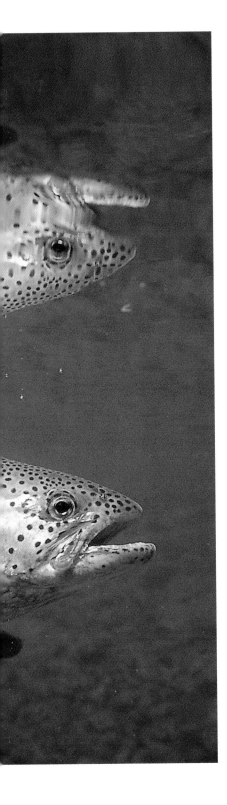

Contents

Getting ready to fish Crowley Lake as the early-morning mist lifts.

Introduction

The inclination of most fly-line anglers in California is to fish moving water. That's a shame, because there are bigger trout in this state's lakes and reservoirs.

It's all very logical. Trout in stillwaters don't have to work as hard fighting currents as those in streams and rivers. Many lakes are extremely rich in insect life, not to mention minnows, so there is plenty of food for trout. The result: In the best of the California lakes, trout just cruise around slurping up food and getting bigger and bigger and bigger.

So why are you still fishing for small trout in small streams?

Don't answer that! I do it, too, and thoroughly enjoy small-stream fishing. But there comes a time in the life of a serious angler, fly-line aficionado or not, when catching big fish becomes important. My intention in this book is to give you the basics of how to do it and to tell you where the best public stillwater fly fishing for trout in California can be found.

Picking the best fishing depends on much more than just the angling. There's the scenery, the atmosphere of the area, all the things that go together to make up the experience. Then there are my own biases, which, despite efforts to be non-judgmental, certainly creep into what I write. It's hard to forget a great day on a specific body of water, even when that water is not usually so generous to anglers.

And there is the question of how to determine the best of anything. It is only fair that you should know the general guidelines that photographer Rick E. Martin and I used to pick what lakes to write about and photograph.

First, it is hard for me to get excited about put-and-take lakes that offer nothing more than stocked hatchery trout. However, in many cases, stocked trout are the base for what becomes a fine fishery. Davis, Eagle, and Crowley Lakes are examples. Some of these planted trout are able to survive for years, growing steadily larger, so although they may have started life in a concrete pen, they flourish in the wild to become wily monsters that are tough to catch.

In other lakes, trout, stocked or wild, may have access to feeder streams that allow spawning. Often there isn't enough breeding habitat to keep a healthy trout population by itself, but it does guarantee a good mixture of hatchery and wild trout for the angler.

Another criterion is access. There are some fine lakes for hiking anglers, but this book sticks to stillwaters that for the most part can be reached by road. There are exceptions, such as Kirman Lake, that require some hiking, but even these bodies of water don't demand a strenuous, multiday, or even multihour journey to and fro. However, when reporting on specific areas, in some cases we do mention the best of the hike-in lakes in the vicinity. It's up to you whether you want to try them.

Then there is the question of size and depth. Realistically, big, deep lakes generally aren't the best bet for fly-line anglers. Sure, there are lots of trout in Lake Shasta and Lake Tahoe, and under certain circumstances and at certain times of year, they can be caught on a fly. But why spend time dredging difficult water when within an hour's drive of either lake there is first-rate stillwater fishing?

The same holds true for the many reservoirs that grace the foothills of the Central Valley. They have trout, but except for the spring or fall, when the fish usually are in the shallows, the trout hold deep because of the hot temperatures that warm the surface water.

Now if you want to fish for bass ... but that's another book.

Geography also plays a role. There isn't much in the way of trout fishing in Southern California. Nor is the west slope of the Sierra Nevada as productive as the nutrient-rich east slope. The logical result: The best trout lakes for the most part are in Northern California and on the east slope of the Sierra.

Last of all, I blushingly admit that I don't know everything about every trout lake in California. Numerous first-rate fly fishers, some of them guides, some of them just folks who love to fish, have been invaluable in providing information for this book. Even when dealing with lakes that I know well and have fished for years, I quizzed other anglers who fish them regularly. In some cases, these anglers are quoted by name, particularly when their name is synonymous with a body of water, like Jay Fair and Eagle Lake. Not only is it proper to give them credit, but it also gives you, the reader, a chance to hear what they say about the lake in their own words.

Interested? Then come join the hunt for big fish in California stillwaters.

Chapter 1

Wild trout

As you read through the chapters on fishing, you'll find a preoccupation with wild trout. So let's take a look at what that means.

There are more than 3,580 cold-water lakes in California. As the new millennium begins, only 20 of them, fewer than 1 percent, are included in the California Department of Fish and Game's Wild Trout, Catch-and-Release, or Heritage Trout Programs.

Historically, the DFG is a strong proponent of put-and-take fishing – toss in truckloads of hatchery-bred

environment that will sustain the trout. In some cases, planting is used to help sustain a fishery – but usually hatchery-born wild-trout fry are used, rather than generic stockers.

The next step came in 1979, when the California Legislature passed the Trout and Steelhead Conservation and Management Planning Act, which added what is known as the Catch-and-Release Program to the Wild Trout Program. This allows the DFG to designate streams or lakes as "catch-

hooked that deeply is almost impossible. It will surely die, even though it may swim away.

This law also mandates that the DFG add 25 miles of streams or rivers and one lake to one or both of the programs each year. Despite good intentions on the part of the DFG, this has been done sporadically, particularly in the case of lakes. It has been much more difficult to identify stillwater fisheries that qualify for special action than it has been to find appropriate streams and rivers.

Act 3 came in 1998, with the Heritage Trout Waters Program for California's native trout, which deals with restoration, conservation, and angling. The streams and lakes in this program must be located within the historic range of the native trout involved.

Brown trout, though not native, have become ubiquitous in Western waters.

trout, and then let anglers catch them and eat them. For generations, that was pretty much where the bulk of the department's revenue went.

In 1971, a handful of dissidents within the DFG, strongly supported by such interested outsiders as California Trout, were able to start the Wild Trout Program, which set aside a handful of streams and lakes reserved for wild trout. The guidelines provide that such waters should be accessible to the public and that they should be able to provide breeding areas and an aquatic

and-release" areas, which in this case means that although there is a zero-take trout limit on some waters, others have provisions allowing anglers to keep either one or two trout, sometimes with a size or slot limit. So "catch-and-release" doesn't always really mean what it says – it can mean "limited take."

Normally, only barbless hooks are allowed, and only flies and lures can be used in these areas – no bait. The reason is that when a trout takes bait, it swallows it deeply and is hooked in the gullet, rather than in the lip. Trying to release a trout

These three programs often overlap, particularly the Wild Trout and Catch-and-Release Programs, with several waters belonging to both. At the turn of the millennium, the DFG counted three lakes in the Wild Trout Program, nineteen in the Catch-and-Release Program, and two in the Heritage Trout Program. In reality, only twenty lakes are involved, because a number of them are in more than one category.

Wild trout and native trout aren't necessarily the same thing. For example, brown trout, brook trout, and lake trout are not native species – they were introduced into California waters more than a century ago, but have become, in many cases, wild trout that are born, bred, and survive on their own. California's native trout include eleven species and subspecies – coastal rainbows (including steelhead), Volcano Creek golden trout, Little Kern goldens, Kern River rainbows, Lahontan cutthroats, Paiute cutthroats, coastal cutthroats, Eagle Lake rainbows, upper McCloud

Lahontan cutthroat are one of California's native trout and are abundant in only a few streams and lakes.

River redbands, Goose Lake redbands, and Warner Valley redbands. Bull trout, which were native to the McCloud River, no longer exist in California.

Native trout, on the other hand, may not be wild. For example, Eagle Lake rainbows have no place to spawn in their native water (although that may change), so they are bred in hatcheries and then put into Eagle Lake as fry or larger fish. They also are planted extensively in other waters all over California because they are a hardy game fish that thrives pretty much everywhere.

To me, wild trout, both native and otherwise, are a precious resource to be preserved. Even when regulations permit it, I have difficulty killing a trout that has overcome tremendous odds to survive and grow in a rushing stream or mountain lake.

This is a trait I believe is shared by most fly fishers. Our game is in the catching, not the keeping.

Some of California's special-regulations lakes are prime fisheries that can be easily reached and warrant major attention, while others offer only mediocre fishing or require a fair amount of hiking. In any case, I've made it a point to include all these lakes in this book, even though some have a chapter to themselves and others rate only a couple of paragraphs.

Lakes that currently are part of the Wild Trout, Catch-and-Release, and Heritage Trout Waters Programs include the following.

NORTHERN CALIFORNIA

Stone Lagoon: Catch-and-Release, Chapter 6

Grass Valley Creek Reservoir: Catch-and-Release, Chapter 7

Manzanita Lake: Catch-and-Release, Chapter 8

Big Lake: Catch-and-Release, Chapter 9

Eastman Lake: Catch-and-Release, Chapter 9

Eagle Lake: Heritage Trout, Chapter 10

THE WEST SLOPE OF THE SIERRA NEVADA

Milton Reservoir: Catch-and-Release, Chapter 14

THE EAST SLOPE OF THE SIERRA NEVADA

Martis Lake: Wild Trout, Catch-and-Release, Chapter 14

Heenan Lake: Catch-and-Release, Heritage Trout, Chapter 15

Kirman Lake: Catch-and-Release, Chapter 16

Roosevelt Lake: Catch-and-Release, Chapter 16

Lane Lake: Catch-and-Release, Chapter 16

McLeod Lake: Catch-and-Release, Chapter 17

Laurel Lakes (two lakes): Wild Trout, Catch-and-Release, Chapter 17

Crowley Lake: Catch-and-Release, Chapter 17

Cottonwood Lakes (four lakes): Catch-and-Release, Chapter 17

Chapter 2

How to fish a lake

There's a fly-fishing phobia somebody once aptly called "fear of frog water." It goes like this: You stand on the shore with your float tube, pontoon boat, or pram, looking at the calm surface of a multi-acre body of water where there purportedly are lurking trout, wondering, "How the hell am I supposed to figure out where the fish are?" There are no visible seams, no riffles, no runs, no pools – none of that stuff that gives you a hint where to drop a fly in moving water.

In reality, there are indications where fish might be hanging out. You just have to know what to look for, and much of it is not the same as in moving water. What I'm offering here is a primer, a quick once-over for those who haven't done much lake fishing. If you want to get deeper into the how-to aspects of frog-water angling, there are numerous excellent books on the market offering detailed instruction on fly fishing stillwaters (a couple of them are listed below).

A major thing to remember is that trout rarely cruise around in the middle of a lake like a teenager practicing driving in an empty parking lot. There are reasons for a trout to be where it is, and those reasons are food, safety, and, sometimes, better-oxygenated or cooler water.

Deep water means less food. Aquatic plants need sunlight to grow, so if they aren't close enough to the surface to get that sunlight, they don't grow. Aquatic insects eat plants, and fish eat insects. Ergo, look for fish in areas where they'll find food, and that means in areas shallow enough for plants to grow – the so-called "littoral zone." Although this area can be as deep as thirty feet, it generally is shallower because lack of clarity in the water keeps the sunlight from penetrating. Minnows, another food for big fish, use plants for protection, so they'll be in there too.

Obviously, shallows are found

Scoping out a lake from a vantage point will pinpoint channels and other likely fishy areas. This is Red Lake near Markleeville.

along the banks of lakes, so banks are a logical place to fish, particularly those with weed growth or structure. The same holds true for islands. Not so obvious are underwater hills or mounds that come close enough to the surface to stimulate plant growth, but may not be visible from the shore. In addition, the sloping sides offer some structure for trout, which they use as protection.

And speaking of protection, here's part two of why trout are where they are. Danger in the trout world comes from above, mostly from birds or a few mammals that feed on fish – unless, of course, it comes from a big brother that munches a little trout. So, as they do in a stream, trout prefer to hang out someplace where they feel safe or can feed, but quickly dash to safety if danger threatens. Safety can be found in deeper water, weeds, or structure such as rocks or a fallen log that can offer them a hiding place.

For this reason, you generally don't find trout wandering around in shallow, barren water, although as with everything else, there can be exceptions. I had a great day fishing mud flats on Lake McCumber, not far from Redding. The trout were searching for food in clear water only a foot or two deep – it was just a matter of spotting one, casting in front of it, then twitching the nymph to get its attention. It was just like targeting bonefish at Christmas Island and just as exciting.

Then there is the question of oxygen, which trout need to survive. Warmer water holds less oxygen, which is why trout tend to stay deeper in lakes during the summer. Water at 67 or 68 degrees Fahrenheit will make trout start to get uncomfortable. Cooler water sinks, and trout will hold in this water, sometimes making forays into warmer water if the bugs are there. They also will stay in inlets, because moving water picks up oxygen, or near underground springs that are pumping cold, oxygenated water into a lake.

In deeper lakes, water tempera-

The prize – who cares who caught it!

tures create what are known as "thermoclines" and "turnover." These factors are perhaps more important to the bait-and-lure angler who regularly fishes deep, but sometimes they'll affect you, too, so bear with me for a brief explanation of what they mean.

In deep lakes, as the surface warms during the spring and summer, the water can form into layers, with the warmest on top, a cooler middle portion, and then the coldest at the bottom. The thermocline is the middle section. (The top section is the "epilimnion" and the bottom the "hypolimnion," but nobody besides scientists ever use these terms.) It is the upper level that has the most circulation, the most food, and the most oxygen. But here's the negative from the trout's point of view: It also becomes the warmest on hot days.

Trout stay in the upper level for food and oxygen, but dip into the cooler thermocline when the surface water becomes too hot, although they generally don't remain there, because the thermocline doesn't hold as much oxygen. They almost never will be found in the deepest section, since there is no food and little oxygen. Experienced anglers try to pinpoint

exactly where the thermocline begins and fish just above it, because trout hold there.

Turnover occurs in all lakes during the fall, as water temperatures become less differentiated from top to bottom. As the upper and middle layers cool, all the water, rather than just the top layer, begins to circulate, or turn over. Because the water mixes, it is pretty much the same temperature everywhere. Because there no longer are defined layers, the areas where trout can be found no longer depend on a thermocline.

By the way, there also is a turnover during the spring in those lakes that freeze over. While the surface of a lake is frozen (32 degrees), the water below will be a few degrees warmer. But when ice-out comes, the temperature stabilizes, and the lake water mixes. This brings up food that has been resting on the bottom, which is one of the reasons ice-out generally brings excellent fishing on mountain lakes.

When approaching a new lake, take the time to scope it out. Do it from the shore, if there is no alternative, but better yet, find a high point overlooking the lake. It is amazing how often you can make a mental map, pinpointing channels, underwater structure, and weed

Steve Ottesen tops off his float tube. That second bladder is more than a back rest – it is a crucial backup if the main bladder fails.

beds. And there's always a distinct possibility of actually spotting fish that can't be seen from water level. Be sure to make mental notes, or even take the time to sketch a rough map, so that once you are on the water, you'll know exactly where you want to be.

When reading a lake, here are the keys to determining where the fish should be.

Above and Below – A rule to remember is that what happens with the terrain above the water generally continues below the water. In other words, a rocky point running down the hillside and into the water almost certainly will continue once it is underwater. If an above-water bank is steep or gradual, chances are it will continue that way. The reason is simple – many lakes are created by man-made dams that filled up a canyon, meadow, or other depression in the terrain.

Inlets – One of the best bets on any lake is where a river, creek, or even a spring runs in. This moving water carries food and allows a trout to hold in one position and wait for dinner to come to it, rather than cruise around looking for edibles.

And when the lake water begins to heat up in the summer, the water coming in may be a bit cooler and hence more comfortable for fish. Even if it is the same temperature, the moving water by its very movement picks up more of the oxygen the trout needs.

In addition, in lakes, trout, whether wild or hatchery-bred, will be looking for flowing water for spawning – rainbows in the spring, browns in the fall. Many inlet streams are too small to accommodate spawning trout, but the fish will hold at the inlet like bachelors at a singles bar, hoping for some action. Naturally, this is a great time for anglers, since these fish can be really packed into a small area.

When fishing inlets, stay far enough away not to spook the fish. If possible, cast from the side, putting your fly into the moving water where it enters the lake, and then let it drift with the current, just as if you were fishing a creek.

On popular fly-fishing lakes such as Martis Creek Reservoir near Truckee or Heenan Lake in the Markleeville area, just about everybody who fishes them is aware of such hot spots. The result can be a

lineup of anglers in float tubes, almost shoulder to shoulder, casting into the inlet – and sometimes across each other's line.

Channels – Many underwater lake channels are a continuation of feeder streams or rivers. Because a majority of lakes in California are artificial impoundments, their waters cover what once were streambeds. Although some channels silt in and disappear over time, others retain their original character and offer trout deeper water where they can hide and make forays into shallow areas for food. Sometimes the shallower water alongside a channel becomes choked with weeds, and only the channel is clear. Like inlets, these are best fished as a moving stream, with particular attention to the edge of the channel.

Weed Beds – These are the life blood of the lake angler. If there is any one rule to remember, it is that where there are weed beds, there are likely to be trout. Weed beds harbor a plentiful supply of both bugs and smaller fish, while at the same time affording protection if a trout senses danger. Pick just about any of the better big-fish trout lakes (Martis, Heenan, Crowley, and Eagle Lakes come to mind) and weed beds will play an important role in where to fish. Usually, the preferred way to work such water is to sit off the weeds in your float tube and cast your fly tight against the edge of the bed. When possible, position yourself so you can work your fly right along the weeds, because the trout will be cruising those areas looking for anything that signals food.

Channels into the weed beds also are prime lies, as are open areas, with or without a channel. The problem with fishing weed beds is that getting your fly tangled in the weeds is a constant threat. In addition, once you hook a trout, you can't allow it run into the weeds, because breaking off is almost certain. Stout leaders that can be used to put the maximum pressure on fish are the best answer. If a trout does get into the weed beds and wraps your leader in the weeds, a trick that sometimes works is to leave a slack line. On occasion, a trout, feeling the lack of pressure, will come out of the weeds the same way it went in, and you'll have another chance at landing it.

Springs – Underwater springs are good trout water for two reasons. Often they carry minerals that stimulate aquatic growth, so there will be bug-rich weeds around them, and when the water temperature of a lake heats up, springs push out a constant flow of cold water that is usually rich in oxygen. The trick, of course, is to locate a spring. Wherever information on underwater springs is available, it is included on the maps in this book, and usually in the text, too. Many lakes have springs that aren't marked, however. One way to look for them is a constant flow of bubbles. Another indication of a spring is a change in the water temperature. If you are float tubing and feel a definite change in temperature on your legs, it's a good possibility that it is caused by a spring. Be sure to do some investigating and pick out a couple of landmarks that will help you find it again.

Drop-offs and Structure – "Structure" is the angler's word for just about any piece of underwater terrain that isn't flat. It can be an island, a sunken log, pilings, depressions, mounds – anything that is a bit different from the surrounding area. Several specific forms of structure have been detailed above, along with why they are important areas for finding fish. Just remember that anything unusual in a lake can be a spot to fish. As they do in creeks and rivers, trout in lakes will hang out around trees and brush that are in or just above the water, seeking the protection they offer. Trees, or even big rocks that have fallen into the water, also are great places to find trout – the trick is casting near or even into a maze of dead branches without getting tangled up.

Drop-offs are prime trout territory because they afford an opportunity for the fish to hold safely in deeper water and make forays into shallower areas where there are more insects for them to eat.

Fishing tips
Some things to remember while fishing lakes

■ **Unlike angling in moving water, stillwater fly fishing requires that you provide the action for your flies.** Generally, that involves stripping your line at varying speeds, but it also can be done by trolling from a float tube, pontoon boat, or even a pram. As a result, it is important to understand the fly you are fishing, what it represents, and how the natural acts. For example, you shouldn't strip a midge pattern fast – that's not the way the natural acts. Nor does it do much good to let a baitfish imitation just sit there.

■ **The most common mistake stillwater anglers make is stripping too fast.** Most naturals move slowly, and that's how you should move most flies. Strips of only an inch or two have to be part of your arsenal, something that's often frustrating and/or just plain boring. On the other hand, it is the way to catch fish.

■ **The pause during stripping is crucial.** As often as not, fish will take a fly during a pause in the strip. Almost every bug you are imitating will swim a bit and then pause to rest. In many cases, a nymph making its way to the surface will sink back down a ways during this pause, which is what your fly will do, too.

■ **Stay in contact with your fly.** Many takes are gentle, and if you don't have a tight line, you'll never know a trout slurped that sucker. You can't keep a tight line if your rod tip is in the air – keep it right above the water or even in the water. On windy days, in particular, putting the rod tip in the water is the best way to go, because it keeps the wind from blowing the line and affecting your strip.

■ **When fishing an underwater slope, try to fish up the slope.** If you are at the deep portion of the slope, casting into shallower water, your fly is spending less time in fishy water than if you are in the shallower water casting out. Trout hold close to the bottom, and that's where you want your fly to be.

■ **Keep track of the wind direction**, particularly during a stiff breeze. The wind blows insects to the downwind shore, and often fish will gather there to take advantage of the congregation. Winds also cause seams on the surface, particularly when there is a slick. Trout will hang out in the choppier water, but move into the slick to feed, so put your fly along these lake-top seams.

■ **If you aren't getting hits, don't keep doing the same thing.** Give a particular tactic ten minutes or so, then change. The change can be to a different retrieve, a different fly, or fishing at a different depth, or it can be just plain moving to another area.

SUGGESTED READING

A book that offers detailed information on how to fish lakes and reservoirs is *Fly-Fishing Stillwaters for Trophy Trout*, by Denny Rickards. It costs $34.95 in hard-cover and is published by Stillwater Productions, P.O. Box 470, Fort Klamath, Oregon 97626.

Another book is *The Fish Bum's Guide to Catching Larger Trout*, written and illustrated by Mike Croft. A softcover book that costs $14.95, it is in a much less serious vein, with cartoon illustrations. At first glance it would seem to be for beginners only, but in fact it is full of good information presented in a light-hearted manner. It is published by Frank Amato Publications, P.O. Box 82112, Portland, Oregon 97282, telephone (503) 653-8108.

Chapter 3

On the water

The answer to your first question is: No, there isn't any graceful way to get into a donut-shaped float tube and enter the water. I've used one for a couple of decades, and although I've become more adept over the years, entering and leaving lakes still makes onlookers giggle.

You can either grin and bear it or buy an open-ended U-shaped or V-shaped tube, which makes getting into and out of the water easier. An alternative is a pontoon boat, of which there now are models of all sizes and shapes. What you buy depends on how you will use it and how much you are willing to pay.

Fishing small lakes and ponds, or even big lakes, if you stay close to your put-in spot, can be done easily with a cheap tube. But long hauls on big lakes are tough if you have to kick all the way, so you might want to consider putting out the money for a pontoon boat with oars, or even a small skiff or pram, if it suits your needs. Just remember that some lakes don't permit boats at all, while others ban gas motors, but do allow use of an electric motor.

No matter what type of float tube or pontoon boat you use, they are to my mind the most effective way to fish most lakes. They are quiet, without the hull noise of a boat. An angler whose lower body is in the water presents a low profile that doesn't spook fish, although the sitting or semi-reclining position required by a tube does call for a bit more work when casting for distance. Small boats and prams solve that problem, but bring others instead. There are pros and cons to all the various options.

There is no graceful way to get into a donut-shaped float tube.

Prams and small boats can be used for fly fishing lakes, but they are noisy in the water and not as maneuverable as float tubes.

DONUT-SHAPED FLOAT TUBES

Pro: Cheap and durable because the bladder usually is the inner tube for a truck tire. The front section is a great place to rest your elbows while doing that slow, slow strip crucial to successful lake fishing. Because half the angler's body is below the surface, the angler presents a low profile to fish, and the part of the body below the water doesn't seem to scare most trout. There is very little noise from water lapping against the rubber and fabric. Anglers are close to the surface, which makes it easy to see what is happening with any bugs in the water.

Con: This is the most awkward of the personal flotation devices. It takes practice to get in and out while wearing fins. Although tough to turn over, they are hard to get out of

when you're in trouble. Anglers can become chilled in cold weather, despite thermal garments under their waders. Casting requires some practice, because fly fishers are low in the water. The rubber bladder is heavy and hard to fill.

U-SHAPED OR V-SHAPED FLOAT TUBES

Pro: Much easier to use while entering or leaving the water, because they are set up so that all you have to do is sit down in them, rather than thread your fin-covered feet through the center hole. They also are lighter, because they use special bladders, rather than heavy inner tubes. They are easier to get out of in case of trouble. For hiking or backpacking, lightweight tubes can be a blessing, particularly those that can be easily inflated. Other advantages are the same as

with donut-shaped tubes.

Con: No place to rest your arms while stripping. They cost more. Other negatives are the same as for round tubes.

PONTOON BOATS

Pro: Easier to move through the water, and most can be driven either with fins or with oars, which can help cover territory on a large body of water. Because your body is almost entirely out of the water, it is easier to keep warm when the water or weather is cold. Pontoons offer more room for storage, and some even have areas behind the seat that will hold a small cooler.

Con: More expensive, heavier, and bulkier that float tubes. You aren't quite as close to the water, which makes a surprising amount of difference when studying bug action on the surface.

BOATS AND PRAMS

Pro: Much more comfortable than float tubes or pontoon boats, and you can fish with a partner. You don't need to wear waders or fins and can cast standing up. Plenty of room for a cooler, extra rods, and other gear. Easy to cover territory on a big body of water, particularly on lakes that allow the use of a gas engine.

Con: Water noise caused by the hull, particularly with metal boats, scares fish. Boats are not as maneuverable, and you can't control them nearly as well as a float tube, particularly in tight areas where you need to hold in a specific spot despite wind or current. Anglers are not close to the water, which makes it difficult to see insect action. Even with lightweight prams or other small boats, you need to be able to get close to the shoreline to put them in the water.

Since most anglers choose some kind of float tube or pontoon boat for lakes fishing, here are some pointers for float tubers, broken down into sections on safety, equipment, and helpful hints.

SAFETY

Above all, be safe. Most tubes have two bladders, the second usually functioning as a back rest, so there is a backup in case the main tube deflates. It may be tough making it back to shore with only a small bladder keeping you afloat, but it is better than having no backup bladder at all. It certainly doesn't hurt to have a life vest, either. The easiest to use is the type that can be inflated with a self-contained CO_2 cartridge – they go over your shoulders like suspenders and don't get in the way while fishing. If your tube doesn't have a backup bladder, you absolutely must wear some kind of flotation device. No fish is worth drowning for.

Be realistic and give yourself enough time to get back to land and to your car before it gets pitch black. If dusk falls, the other side of a lake isn't the place to be, and keeping your bearings while finning backward in the dark is tough to do. Don't put yourself in that position.

Carry a full-sized flashlight. You may not intend to be on the water after dark, but sometimes such things happen. It also doesn't hurt to include a whistle as part of your tubing gear. Things can go dreadfully wrong on the water, and a whistle probably will bring help quicker than shouting.

When fishing after dark, such as during the *Hexagenia* hatch on Lake Almanor, wear the type of flashlight that has a headband. (You still need to bring a full-sized flashlight.) They throw light where you are looking and leave both hands free, a must for changing flies.

It is tough to turn a float tube over, but it can be done, and people drown in tubes every year. If you can, particularly if you are a first-time tuber, try out your rig in a swimming pool with somebody there to help you. A key to safety in a round float tube is that if it is overturned, the only way you are going to get out of it is to go down. You can't get upright again while you are in the tube, so swim downward until you are clear and then come up outside the tube. Getting your fins through the holes in the seat is awkward, but unsnapping the buckle between the two leg holes before trying to get out helps. That's easier said than done if you are upside down in the water and probably near panic, but these are things you need to think about beforehand.

EQUIPMENT

Float Tubes – Unless you need the exercise, don't try to pump up a tube by hand with a bicycle pump. It'll take you forever. Fill it at a service station or invest in one of those little electric pumps that can be plugged into the cigarette lighter of a vehicle. It takes a long time, too, but at least you can be rigging up and putting on your waders while it does the job. There also are various types of hand pumps, but they work a lot better with special bladders made for U and V tubes than with the truck tire inner tube that provides flotation for most of the donut-shaped belly boats.

Filling a tube properly takes some practice. It needs to be filled

tight enough to fill the fabric entirely, but not so tight that it stretches the fabric and rips a seam. If you are filling a tube at a lower altitude and then driving up into the mountains, remember that the higher you go, the less outside air pressure there is, so the tube will expand. If you forget and go high, your tube will expand enough to rip some seams or even explode. If headed up, underfill the tube and top it off near your destination, if need be. On the other hand, once you put the tube in a cold mountain lake, the air in the tube cools, and the pressure drops. The result can be a slightly underinflated tube.

Waders – Wear chest waders, not waist-high waders. Waist-highs may appear enough to keep you dry

Pontoon boats, also known as kick boats, are fast replacing float tubes as the most popular method of fishing stillwaters.

when you get in the water, but the slightest bit of wave action, or even kicking along fairly fast, can bring water in over the top. This I know from experience – I once had to cut short a great day of lake fishing because water came in over my waist-high waders, thoroughly soaking and chilling me. For the record, I was wearing the shorter waders because I brought the wrong wader bag.

Also, the bottom pockets of a full-length fishing vest will get wet in a float tube so use a "shortie" vest, take stuff out of the bottom pockets of a full-length vest, or just skip the vest altogether and stash whatever you need in the pockets of the float tube.

Fins – I usually avoid recom-mending a specific product, but Force Fins are a favorite with float tubers. They have a short, curved surface that makes them one of the easiest fins to walk in, and they give you a powerful stroke. The negative is that they are expensive, costing as much as an entry-level float tube. If you buy them, make certain you get the foot size large enough to fit over whatever you plan to wear in the water, since the toe hole isn't adjustable in the less-expensive model. And be sure to invest a few more bucks on a tether that will hold them to your ankles, because if they come loose, they sink!

Rods – Some people insist that heavier rods such as an 8-weight or 9-weight are the best bet while tub-ing because they offer more back-bone and allow you to make longer casts. Other anglers are addicted to light 3-weight or 4-weight rods. I prefer to use a 9-foot 5-weight or 6-weight because it allows for longer casts and has enough backbone to fight good-sized fish. Most of us practice catch-and-release fishing, and that mandates bringing a fish to the net quickly enough so it will not be overly tired.

In reality, just about any rod will do if you haven't got a lot of gear and don't want to invest in new equip-ment for lake fishing. However, if you really get into it and want prop-er gear in your hunt for large still-water fish, a rod with a soft tip, but with backbone is the way to go. The soft tip allows more feel when a big fish oh-so-gently slurps a size 20

Consider taking two rods. Although most stillwater fishing is done with a sinking or sink-tip line, there are times when the action is on the top. Usually, dry-fly action doesn't last that long, and time spent changing a reel or line can eat up precious moments.

midge, and it takes more of the shock when the lunker suddenly discovers it's hooked and makes a desperate dash. The backbone, of course, is for landing that lunker.

Nets – If you want to land a fish, rather than just take the hook out of its mouth in the water, use a net. Trying to reach a fish with a long leader can be difficult, and a net is an indispensable aid. The net also helps the fish, presuming you practice catch-and-release angling, by not subjecting it to a scraping on the hard fiber material of the float tube, not to mention avoiding the grappling and squeezing necessary to deal with a flopping trout. I prefer a wood-frame net (it floats!), hooked to the left-hand side of the tube (I'm right-handed). I use a magnet tether that holds it tight to the tube when not in use and when entering and leaving the water, but that allows it

to be broken loose so I can reach out for a fish. The longer the handle, the easier it is to net a fish, particularly for short-armed guys like me.

Other Gear – Many times there is the problem of getting to the water from where you've filled the tube and rigged up. Chances are you'll be using stocking-foot waders, and rocks not only can hurt your feet, but also can cut the neoprene of the waders. Rubber flats boots are great for tubing, but you need to take their bulk into account when buying flippers (or take them off once you are ready to get into the water). The same is true with slip-over neoprene socks that can be put on over your wader feet. A less-expensive way to deal with the problem is to buy an oversized pair of cheap tennis shoes that slip on over your waders while walking and that can be taken off and stuffed into a float tube pocket while on the water.

Most fly shops also carry little anchors, usually weighing either one-and-a-half or three pounds, that can come in handy when you find a hot spot. Just a slight breeze or current can quickly move you away from where you want to be, and it's a pain to have to turn around and paddle back into position, not to

mention the fishing time lost. It also is hard to do the very slow retrieves that are the bread and butter of lake fishing when you are being moved by the wind or current.

HELPFUL HINTS

■ I always string my rod and put some sort of fly on before I get in the water. I also am extremely careful of the rod while getting into or out of the water. There's a school of thought that maintains it is easier to break the rod into two pieces and then put it together once you are in the water. Certainly the rod is easier to hold that way, and it doesn't stick out as much.

■ If you have to change a line or deal with a fouled tip while in the water, just drop the butt of the rod into the water and let it sink straight down until you can safely handle the rod without bending it. Don't try to bend the rod to deal with the tip or to string a line, because you may end up with a three-piece rod that started as a two-piece rod. And don't forget to hang on to that puppy when you have most of it sunk in the water and you are fooling around with the tip. Rods don't float.

■ Consider taking two rods. Although most stillwater fishing is done with a sinking or sink-tip line, there are times when the action is on the top. Usually, dry-fly action doesn't last that long, and time spent changing a reel or line can eat up precious moments. The usual drill is to have one rod with a floating line, the other with a sinking or

John King does it the old-fashioned way – by wading.

sink-tip line. However, there may be times when it is more effective to have one rod with a slow-sinking line and a second with a medium or fast-sinking line. My suggestion is that novice float tubers stick with one rod until they are comfortable with their setup. A second rod definitely is something else to worry about while on the water, and you need to figure out a way to keep from getting tangled while stripping or fighting a fish.

■ It may seem obvious, but if you get in your tube on the bank and then move toward the water, walk backward. It's pretty hard to walk forward with fins, and you could trip and fall, doing damage to yourself or your rod. Just pick up the float tube by the handles on each side and step slowly backward. There is no way to be graceful doing this so don't worry about it. In slick mud, on rocks, or near sharp drop-offs, it isn't easy, so take your time.

If you're fishing with a friend, don't hesitate to ask for a steadying hand or to be handed your rod after you get settled in the water. Here's an important safety pointer: Once you get into the water, don't just drop the tube and sit down backward. If you are in shallow water, the force of flopping heavily into the tube could turn it over. Make certain you are in well above your knees and then sit down gently.

■ Again the obvious: To get somewhere in the water, you go backward. If there is some distance to go, try to get a reference point the way you are facing, so that you don't have to turn and look over your shoulder constantly. You'll still have to crane your neck at regular intervals, but perhaps not as often. You also need a reference point behind you, the way you are going, so that you have some idea you are headed for the right spot. It is surprising how far off course even the slightest

wind or current can carry you.

■ Last of all, don't drink coffee when you are going float tubing. Peeing is, if you'll pardon the mixed metaphor, a pain in the butt. Sitting in a tube out in the water wrapped in neoprene and warm underwear is no place to have to go because there is no place to go. I know folks who wear adult diapers when float tubing, but that's your choice. What do I do? I paddle to shore, get out of my tube and do what comes naturally.

One final admonition: Be courteous to other float tubers. When the water is crowded, there usually are a number of tubers slowly trolling back and forth. Stay out of their lanes and don't force them to change direction. Also, stay far enough away from other tubers to allow them room to cast, including room for their back casts. They have a right to the water around them, as do you.

Chapter 4

Bugs and their imitations

Flies for fishing in stillwater aren't necessarily the same as those used in streams and rivers. To begin with, anglers can't toss a Royal Wulff or Humpy onto the surface of a calm lake during a mayfly hatch and expect a big trout to take it. Unlike fish in a fast-moving stream, which must decide in a fraction of a second whether to eat a passing bug, stillwater trout usually have plenty of time to inspect what's on the menu.

Because of this, the successful stillwater angler will present flies that match the hatch and present them in such a way as to imitate the action of the real thing. I'll get into specifics a little later, but here are some generalizations on what to fish and what not to fish.

Stoneflies live in running water, and lakes don't move much. So that eliminates what is a major fish food in most rivers and streams. There are exceptions, where the current in a lake is strong enough to support a stonefly hatch, but these are few and far between.

Baetis mayflies also are stream dwellers. For lakes and reservoirs, it is the *Callibaetis* you'll need to worry about.

Chironomids (midges) play a crucial role in lake fishing, so get used to straining your eyes with size 22 flies. (Actually, in some cases, you can fish them as large as size 12 or 14.)

Damselflies, and to a lesser extent, dragonflies, are a major meat source for lake trout. Make sure you have plenty of imitations on hand, particularly nymphs.

Caddisflies are around in numbers, just as in streams. The same flies work in both places.

Leeches, snails, and even small eels, all of which are key foods in lakes, are imitated by Woolly Buggers and other big, fuzzy flies.

Minnows and other fry may not qualify as "bugs," but they are food for fish. In some lakes, Crowley being a prime example, minnows (Sacramento perch fry) are a major food source, and if you don't fish an imitation, you are going to miss out on catching some lunkers.

There are major works on all aspects of fishing-related entomology, and if you have a strong interest in that part of the game, you'll want to do more study (some suggested reading is listed on Page 27). What follows is just a primer on what bugs and other food items are available to trout in lakes, including a few of the standard imitations and how to fish them.

Size 20 Copper Soft Hackle, an excellent midge imitation.

Hexagenias *are the biggest of the mayflies and grow in only a few lakes or slow-moving rivers with muddy or sandy bottoms.*

MIDGES

All together, fellow anglers: "I hate fishing midges!" Now that we've got that out of our system, let's get on with it.

Midges are a major food source for trout, and unless you can fish them, you'll miss out. For anglers, they have two downsides. First, they often are so small you can't see your fly. Second, the best way to fish them is to just let them sit there, either in the film or just under the surface. That can be as exciting as watching grass grow.

The payoff, of course, is hooking a five-pound fish on a size 22 midge imitation. I didn't say you'd land it, particularly when you have to use a 3-pound or 4-pound tippet, but that exciting possibility is there.

Midges are members of the Chironomidae family, which are part of the order Diptera (the true flies, which includes mosquitoes, bluebottles, and thousands of other varieties) and often are referred to as "chironomids." They hatch all year around, which is what makes them such an important food source for trout, and they live in just about any type of stillwater. They come in a variety of sizes, from as big as size 12 to so small they are impossible to imitate, and in a variety of colors, from red to cream to black. For the most part, they are fished in sizes 18 through 22.

Where there are Blood Midges – so called because of their red color – a Brassie can be a good choice. It sits well in the water, with its tail hanging down in imitation of the natural. The red color is caused by hemoglobin that allows the blood midge to absorb and retain oxygen and thus live and feed in deep, oxygen-poor muddy bottoms. Among many other midge larva and pupa patterns are the San Juan Worm, Dave Whitlock's Midge Larva, and the Mosquito.

For dries, there are a variety of patterns, but the most popular is the Griffith's Gnat, from size 16 to 22, which is simple to tie, even in those small sizes – a peacock herl body with grizzly hackle palmered forward. Simplicity in tying is important, because fishing midges with a light tippet, as usually is necessary, means losing a lot of flies.

Like most aquatic flies, midge nymphs make their way to the surface, hatch, and fly away. But they do it oh-so-slowly, and they do it in huge numbers, which means that getting a trout to take an imitation when it is among a hundred naturals can be tough.

One way to fish a nymph is to put flotant on your tippet up to six or seven inches from the fly. This allows the midge nymph to sink to about that depth. The trouble is that sometimes a trout will gently sip the fly, but you'll have no indication of the take before it spits it out. A more effective way is to drop the nymph from an indicator, which moves when the trout takes the artificial. My preferred way is to drop the nymph from a dry fly and use it as an indicator. You never can tell – maybe the trout will decide on the spur of the moment that it needs something more substantial than a midge.

I also use this technique fishing small dry midges. I may not be able to see the midge imitation, but I can keep my eye on the larger attractor, and if there is a rise in the vicinity, I set the hook.

If a trout is in the area, give the fly an occasional small twitch – just enough to get the fish's attention. If you want to retrieve, do it very, very slowly, only an inch or so at a time.

It's tough fishing this way, and it requires patience. For those whose experience has been on moving water, or for those whose idea of fishing a lake is to troll in a float tube, it can be frustrating and takes some getting used to. The payoff is there because it is a way to catch more and bigger fish.

MAYFLIES

When it comes to mayflies, think *Callibaetis*. That's the so-called Speckled Dun, and the hatch goes from April into October, usually in the late morning and early afternoon. If it is windy, there usually is no hatch, although sometimes *Callibaetis* will hatch in protected coves.

There are progressive hatches during the year, with the flies becoming smaller and smaller. Try about a size 12 in the spring, ending with a size 16 or 18 in the fall.

Imitations are the same as you use on moving water. For nymphs, a Gold-Ribbed Hare's Ear, Pheasant Tail, or Bird's Nest, size 12 to 18. A tan Hare's Ear is probably the closest to the real thing.

Try an Adams or Light Cahill, size 12 to 18, for a dry. If you want to fish a spinner, which usually isn't all that effective on lakes, a Rusty Spinner, size 16 to 20, will do.

Callibaetis nymphs are more active than midges, moving along in a slow, pulsating motion. Get your fly down to where you think the fish are and then retrieve with a strip-strip-pause action, using strips of two or three inches. A reminder: Don't take my suggestions about how to fish these flies as gospel. If a technique isn't catching fish, and you are pretty sure some are around, do something differently. Maybe a long, slow strip will get their attention, or perhaps a slow rise from bottom to top.

CADDISFLIES

Although they are the major food source in California for trout in moving water, caddisflies don't appear to be quite that important in lake fishing. They do play a role, however, and come in a variety of colors, from black to light tan, and in just about every size from 10 to 18.

As with most lake fishing, subsurface flies are more important than dries. Let's face it, when a trout takes your Hare's Ear or Pheasant Tail, is it saying "This is a mayfly nymph" or "This is a caddis pupa"? Who knows? Those ubiquitous flies will pass for either one in a pinch.

Damselflies are prime food for stillwater trout just about anywhere in California.
This version is called a Flash Damsel.

A just-hatched damselfly. They crawl onto anything available, including float tubes, to dry off before their maiden flight.

Of course, you also can use cased caddis imitations, or Green Rock Worms, which imitate caddis larvae. No matter what you use, fish them just like mayfly nymphs, with a slow retrieve and regular pauses.

When it comes to dries, there's nothing wrong with an Elk Hair Caddis, size 12 to 16. Tie them in a range of colors, from black to light tan.

DAMSELFLIES AND DRAGONFLIES

Damselflies are a key trout food. They are pretty much everywhere in stillwaters and are big enough to offer fish a steak-sized meal. An added bonus: Watching the bright-blue insects land on your rod, float tube, or even on you adds something to a day on the water.

I've got a couple of friends who tie beautiful imitations of the adult damselfly. The trouble is, I very seldom catch fish with an adult – it's the nymph that does the job.

Damselflies must crawl onto something to hatch into adults, so when the time comes, they tend to migrate toward shore. Whenever they find something solid, be it reeds, a log, or a float tube, they climb on to make the transformation. The fish know this and move into shallow water to eat the damsel nymphs that are searching for a place to hatch.

When they do hatch, they are a yellow or olive color, and it takes a day or two for them to turn the bright blue (or sometimes green) that makes them so pretty. The nymphs are anywhere from olive to tan, and their color will change even during a day of hatches.

Hatches are in the late spring and summer and occur on sunny days – you won't find them coming off in a rain or during a heavy overcast.

There are any number of damselfly nymph imitations. Most effective ones have one thing in common – they are long and slender and have a tail with plenty of action, often made of marabou. I tie one with a bead head and a bit of Flashabou in the tail.

Usually you don't need to fish damselfly nymph imitations deep, particularly if you are looking for trout that have come into shallow water. You can use a floating or a slow-sinking line to keep them in the first couple of feet of water. Use a fairly slow strip-strip-pause retrieve, and be prepared for a hard take.

Dragonfly nymphs are larger and darker than damsels and are a lot tougher for trout to see. Still, trout go after them during a hatch, when, like damsels, they move into shallow water. Adults for the most part aren't trout food.

A Carey Special, one of my favorite stillwater flies, works well as a dragonfly nymph, as do Woolly Buggers. Fish them right on the bottom with a stripping and pausing action, but the strips can be six or eight inches long and much faster than with a damselfly.

MINNOWS

It is something of a mystery why so few fly-line anglers fish minnow imitations. Big trout are carnivorous and eat smaller fish, including their brethren. Added pluses are that you don't need to worry about a "hatch," and you can haul the streamers that imitate small fish through the water at a reasonable speed – none of those creeping retrieves.

Just about any streamer will work well, as long as it has the general color and size of the baitfish it is imitating. The favored fish foods are threadfin shad, Sacramento perch, sculpins, and shiners. Good imitations include Zonkers, Hornberg Specials, and even flies generally used in salt water, such as small Deceivers or Whistlers.

Strip fast, so the fly looks like a minnow fleeing for its life, and you'll trigger a trout's grab-it instinct. Just remember to use a heavy tippet, or you'll never land a fish, because the take is not a gentle sip.

Andy Burk, one of the better fly fishers around, uses this technique on Martis Lake, near Truckee. He even goes one better by tucking the rod under his arm and stripping as fast as he can with both hands. He doesn't catch that many fish, he says, but the ones he hooks are almost without exception real lunkers.

LEECHES AND SNAILS

These are two fish foods anglers usually don't see, but believe me, they are there and are favorite items on the menus of big trout.

Leeches are long and flexible, just like earthworms, ranging in size from half an inch to several inches. They normally come in dark colors, ranging from black to brown to dark red, and are found on the bottoms of lakes, often in shallow water.

Woolly Buggers work just fine as leech imitations, or you can use a Marabou Leech, size 2 through 10. Whatever you use should have an undulating movement and hold a long, flat shape. Fish these imitations with a pause-strip motion and weight the head so that this will result in an up-and-down action.

If you don't believe that trout eat snails, shells and all, then all you have to do is pick up a big trout on Lake Davis when it is feeding on snails. You can feel a bellyful of snail shells, and if it has been gorging, they will be making bulges in the trout's stomach.

I've seen snail patterns, usually brown or tan material wrapped to give a vaguely circular shape on a hook. I just use a Woolly Bugger or Woolly Worm tied with a lot of chenille. Snails move like, well, snails, so use a slow strip, crawling them along the bottom or through weedy areas. I've been told that snails actually will float to the surface of some lakes, including Eagle Lake, and hang upside down from the underside of the surface film, dropping back to the bottom if there is a disturbance. When that happens, trout

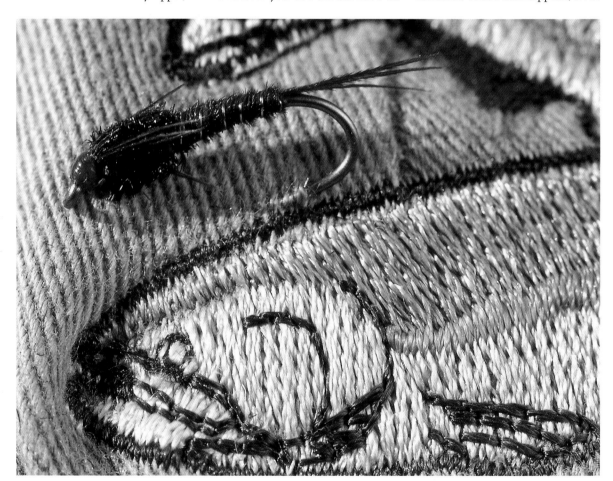

The Pheasant Tail is a top nymph on trout waters, moving or still.

will key on them, and an imitation tossed into the area and allowed to sink will draw a vicious strike. I've never run across this phenomenon, so I can't speak from first-hand experience.

SCUDS

Scuds are little shrimplike crustaceans, and in almost every lake where they exist, trout gorge on them and grow exceptionally fast. Kirman Lake, north of Bridgeport, home to some oversized brook trout, is an example.

Scuds are scavengers that tend to stay in fairly shallow water, where there is plenty of decaying plant and animal matter for them to eat. They don't like sunlight, so they are more active in the morning and evening, or on overcast days.

Artificials usually are tied on curved scud hooks and come in a variety of colors, ranging from olive to pink. There is no generic imitation that can pass for a scud – you'll have to either tie some or buy some. The color and size depends on which lake you are planning to fish, because these little creatures tend to take on the coloring of their habitat.

They can be fished two ways, either with a slow strip-and-pause retrieve or by hanging them just under the surface with an indicator. Because there usually are so many naturals around, I prefer the strip-and-pause method, because it helps call attention to my fly.

TERRESTRIALS

Grasshoppers and other terrestrials don't play as important a role in stillwaters as they do in moving water, although trout occasionally key on them. There are times when the wind is blowing grasshoppers or ants onto the water and the trout go after them with a vengeance. Just keep your eyes open, and if it happens, give them a try.

Remember that the wind will blow anything on the surface to the downwind shore. Trout know this and will move into the area, so if you can paddle over and fish the shoreline where the waves and water movement are stacking up the bugs you'll increase your odds.

The Carey Special, an old wet fly that's back in vogue, is very effective on lakes.

Flies: A baker's dozen

This baker's dozen of flies should cover most situations, as long as you have them in different sizes and colors.

Midges: Brassies, size 14 to 18, for a Blood Midge, plus another midge pattern, size 16 to 22, in cream, tan and olive. For dries, Griffith's Gnats, size 18 to 22.

Nymphs: Gold-Ribbed Hare's Ears, size 12 to 16, light and dark tan; Pheasant Tails, size 12 to 16. (They imitate both mayfly nymphs and caddis pupae.)

Emergers: AP Emergers, size 12 to 16. (They imitate both mayfly and caddis emergers.)

Dries: Use an Adams, size 12 to 18, for *Callibaetis*, and an Elk Hair Caddis, size 12 to 16, for caddisflies.

Damselfly Nymphs: Take your pick of a pattern, but tie it in sizes from 8 to 12 and in colors from dark olive to light tan.

Minnows: Again, pick your pattern, depending on where you are fishing. Hornberg Specials, size 8 to 10, are local favorites to imitate the Sacramento perch that abound in two of the top stillwaters, Crowley Lake and Bridgeport Reservoir.

Leeches and Snails: Woolly Buggers, size 6 to 10, in olive, black, brown, and yellow. They imitate a variety of insects and are a staple when you're searching for fish. Black marabou Leeches, size 6 to 8.

Scuds: A scud pattern, size 10 to 14. Color depends on where you plan to fish.

A Bonus Fly: I couldn't live without the Carey Special, size 10 to 12, an old wet fly that is having a well-deserved resurrection. It is just plain "buggy," and as such imitates all sorts of things. It is an excellent fly to use while searching for fish.

SUGGESTED READING

Suggested reading for those who want to get deeper into the entomology of fly fishing:

The Complete Book of Western Hatches, by Rick Hafele and Dave Hughes, published by Frank Amato Publications, P.O. Box 82112, Portland, Oregon 97282, (503) 653-8108. This is the basic text that covers California and is an excellent starting point.

Caddisflies, by Gary LaFontaine, published by Lyons and Burford, 31 West 21st Street, New York, NY 10010.

Sierra Trout Guide, by Ralph Cutter, published by Frank Amato Publications, P.O. Box 82112, Portland, Oregon 97282, (503) 653-8108.

Selective Trout, by Doug Swisher and Carl Richards, published by New Century Publishers, 220 Old New Brunswick Road, Piscataway, NJ 08854.

Chapter 5

The Alturas area

DODGE BUCKHORN ROUND CORRAL NELSON CORRAL
SMITH BLUE CLEAR BAYLEY SWORINGER
FEE LILY CAVE BRILES BALLARD

The northeastern corner of California is one of the best-kept stillwater fly-fishing secrets around. It's a long drive from everywhere, anglers need to know where they are going, and, let's face it, this isn't the most beautiful country in the Golden State, unless you are a fan of high-plains desert with lots of sagebrush, juniper, jackrabbits, and cattle.

What it does have is numerous impoundments with big fish. That said, let's cut to the nitty-gritty, because anglers need to know up front exactly what to expect before they make the trek to Modoc County and surrounding areas.

First, with a couple of exceptions, you'll be fishing for planted trout. That's not as much a negative as it might seem. Many of the hatchery fish are Eagle Lake strain rainbows, an excellent game fish. Most of the lakes and reservoirs are very rich in food, so a trout planted at ten or twelve inches will be sixteen or even eighteen inches by the time the season opens the next spring – and given decent weather, there can be plenty of holdovers. By their third year in area stillwaters, trout will be pushing twenty inches, and after that ... well, let's just say enough fish from five to nine pounds are landed each year to make it a common occurrence.

Second, the fishing available in these stillwaters depends on the weather during preceding years. Was there enough precipitation and runoff during the winter and spring to fill the reservoir or lake? Has there been enough water for a couple of years or more so the holdovers have had a chance to grow? On the smaller reservoirs, was there a hard winter freeze that killed trout and prevented holdovers?

Third, for the most part, these reservoirs exist because ranchers or government agencies built them, either for irrigation or as watering holes for cattle. They are loaded with algae and sediment, and there are times when the water clarity is so bad you can't see your fins. As a result, many of the best ones are just plain butt-ugly, at least when compared with the pine-bedecked shores of pristine, blue mountain lakes. In addition, ranchers or farmers own the water rights and can empty a prime lake if they feel they need the water. Although most of them are careful to preserve enough water to keep the trout alive, that isn't always the case.

Jackie King on Nelson Corral, a high-desert reservoir that holds some big trout.

The Alturas area is a worm dunker's heaven. With several dozen reservoirs sporting fish, not one of them has special restrictions. And that's the way the locals want it – take your limit (or sometimes more, because Department of Fish and Game wardens are a rarity), even if that's five fish of five pounds each. At the same time, there are constant complaints from the local anglers that "it ain't what it used to be." How they expect to kill every big fish caught and still have big fish in every puddle is a mystery.

A handful of local fly-line anglers, spearheaded by John King, head of the Modoc/Alturas Chapter of Trout Unlimited, have attempted to get some waters into the DFG's Catch-and-Release Program, but so far, efforts have been fruitless, mostly because of the vociferous opposition from the county fish and game commission and some county supervisors. There are no fly-fishing shops in Alturas, nor is there a fly-fishing club to help present the fly fishers' point of view.

The last thing you want to do in this area is expound the virtues of a reduced limit or special restrictions on hooks or bait. Local folks who couldn't be nicer suddenly become sworn enemies, acting as if you are ripping food from the mouths of their babies.

Put this all together and it makes a difficult area about which to write. I can't tell you where to go, because a specific lake that was great last year may have suffered a winter kill or a summer drought that pretty much eliminated any holdover fish. In addition, in several of what used to be prime reservoirs, the tui chub has taken over in such numbers that the trout fishing is mediocre, at best. This situation probably will get worse, rather than better, because the DFG is very limited in how aggressive it can be in getting rid of such nongame fish. At this point, the debacle at Lake Davis in the late 1990s (the lake was poisoned to kill the northern pike that had been illegally introduced, touching off lawsuits and a major battle between locals and the DFG) has pretty much precluded the use of rotenone to poison waters and rid them of unwanted fish that compete with trout or bass.

What I can do is tell you what specific waters are like and how to get there, which is important, because many of them are on unmarked dirt roads deep in the sagebrush. If there has been plenty of water for a couple of years, then most of these reservoirs should be well worth fishing, including the smaller ones. There are a few small impoundments of five or ten acres that can pump out huge fish and

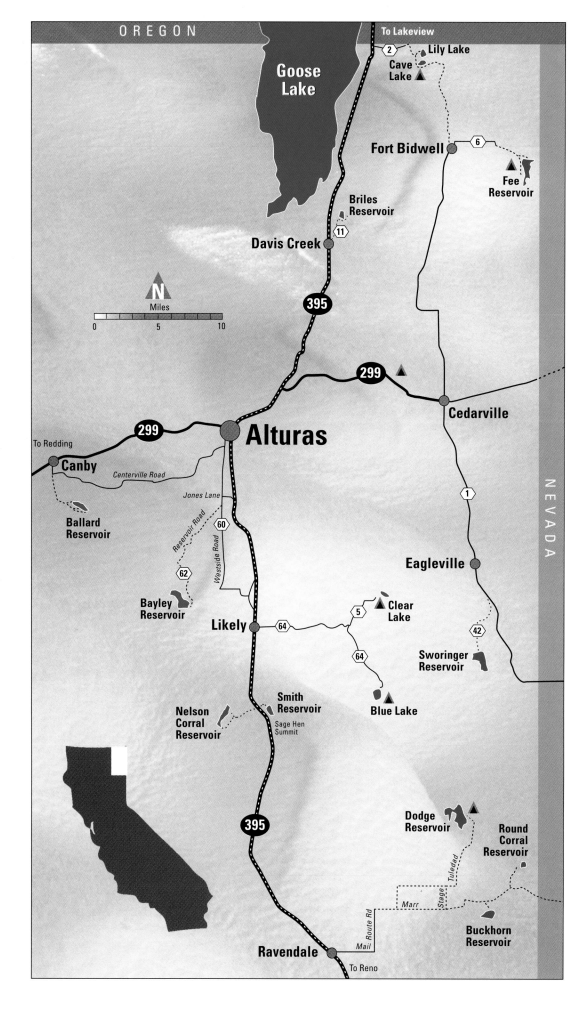

John King trolls for brookies on Briles Reservoir.

often get little pressure. If precipitation has been low, or the winter extra cold, then you'll probably do better sticking to the larger reservoirs, where holdover fish have a better chance of surviving.

If you don't know the area and want to pay a visit, call the sporting-goods stores or the U.S. Forest Service (the telephone numbers are at the end of the chapter) and hear what they have to say about current conditions. If it isn't a disastrous water year, any of these reservoirs should offer good fishing. Give them a try.

HOW TO GET THERE, WHAT TO EXPECT

From most of northern and central California, probably the best way to get to Alturas is to follow Interstate 5 to Redding, then Highway 299 142 miles east to Alturas. An alternate route, or the way to go if you live in the eastern section of California or prefer to take Interstate 80 over the Sierra Nevada, is to follow Highway 395 north 169 miles from Reno.

Alturas is the seat of a county that claims fewer than 10,000 inhabitants, one of the smallest in California. It has a population of about 3,000 people and is in a high plains desert some 4,300 feet above sea level. For years, the Southern Pacific Railroad was the driving economic force, followed by timber. But the railroad is gone, and the timber industry is on a downhill slide, so cattle ranching now is the main industry.

There are few other towns in this part of the world, but Alturas is geared to handle visitors, offering motels, RV parks, and restaurants.

Apart from the fishing, this is a good area for general wildlife viewing. The Modoc National Wildlife Refuge is south of Alturas and hosts a variety of birds, including bald and golden eagles, tundra swans, and sandhill cranes, along with shorebirds, ducks, herons, and egrets. There also are antelope, Rocky Mountain elk, mule deer, and numerous smaller animals.

HOW TO FISH THE ALTURAS AREA

Because most of these stillwaters are pretty much the same, there is no sense in giving a lake-by-lake how-to-fish-it rundown. Here are general guidelines.

The best fishing is in the spring. Not only do you get hungry fish, but most of them are good-sized holdover planters – if you hit the lakes before the DFG dumps the current year's crop of hatchery trout shortly before Memorial Day. The downside is that roads still muddy from winter snow and spring runoff can make getting to some of the lakes difficult, even with a four-wheel-drive vehicle. I'll describe the condition of roads to specific reservoirs, because some of them are tough to reach by family sedan, and a lot of them will give your car a beating.

As summer comes on and the water heats up, the trout become more selective. They also tend to eat in the morning or evening and stay deeper during the hotter part of the day. Fishing from nine or ten in the morning until five or six in the evening can be frustrating, because the trout lurk lethargically in the deeper, cooler parts of a reservoir. The fishing turns on again in the fall, usually in mid-to-late September, when temperatures begin to drop and the water cools.

Trout food is always plentiful, which is why there are big fish. Most of the lakes have just about everything a trout wants to eat – mayflies, caddisflies, leeches, damselflies and dragonflies, scuds, snails, and minnows. If there's a hatch, match it. If there isn't, try generic nymphs such as Pheasant Tails, Hare's Ears, Bird's Nests, or Zug Bugs. In the early summer, damselflies are a prime food, and size 10 nymph imitations can be a killer.

Woolly Buggers and Woolly Worms or leech imitations in olive, cinnamon, brown, or black are always effective. If you like local flies, John King ties what he calls a Midnight Special on a size 12 hook (Mustad 80260). The recipe for this pattern: black thread, a one-eighth-inch black metal bead, two strands of black Krystal Flash for a tail, "Midnight Rainbow" New Age Chenille for the body, $1\frac{1}{2}$ wraps of grizzly hackle for a shoulder.

As you would on most stillwaters, fish the weed beds, coves, and other areas that are likely to produce food. If you must fish at midday, try getting into deeper water, which generally is found close to the dam at any given reservoir.

Wind is an important factor here. Mornings usually are calm, but the wind begins to blow along about noon. Sometimes it drops in the evenings, sometimes it doesn't. Many of these reservoirs are big enough to have whitecaps when the wind is howling, so using a float tube or small pram becomes difficult. Even casting from shore is ineffective unless you can shoot your line downwind.

WHERE TO FISH

Using Alturas as a starting point, what follows covers the fishing from south to north, grouping the lakes and reservoirs that can be reached from a specific highway.

HIGHWAY 395 SOUTH
Dodge, Buckhorn, and Round Corral Reservoirs

These three impoundments are reached from the little town of Ravendale, which is 54 miles south of Alturas on Highway 395. They mark the southern limits of the fishing lakes in this chapter.

The starting point for the three reservoirs – Dodge is the largest, Buckhorn about half that size, and Round Corral only a few acres – is Mail Route Road, which turns east from Ravendale. From that turnoff, Dodge is 26 miles, Buckhorn 20 miles, and Round Corral 25 miles.

From Ravendale, follow Mail Route Road, which is paved, 10 miles to the intersection with Marr Road. Go straight on Marr Road to the intersection with Stage Road, which turns left. Marr goes straight to Buckhorn and Round Corral, while Stage Road leads to Dodge Reservoir. More detail is included under the description of each lake.

Dodge Reservoir: Because it sits at 5,735 feet and is one of the largest of the reservoirs in this chapter, Dodge remains quite fishable when some of the smaller lakes are in trouble due to lack of water. It has a primitive campground (no water) and a dirt boat-launch ramp.

To get there from the Stage Road / Marr Road intersection, turn left on Stage Road. It is a good gravel road, and you can move right along, but watch out for cattle – you may well find them taking a siesta in the middle of the road. At the stop sign (yes, a stop sign!) turn right on County Highway 506 (Tuledad Road), which winds up into the Cottonwood Mountains for about 10 miles to the reservoir.

There is a rough dirt road that goes around most of the lake, which has numerous coves with lots of weed growth. It really is a question of picking a likely spot and giving it a try.

Dodge is heavily stocked with Eagle Lake trout in the expectation that many of them will find enough food to become holdovers. What this means for the angler is that if

Lily Lake is full of stocked rainbows that usually are fished out before they get big.

Briles Reservoir is a pretty, off-the-road water with stocked trout and not many visitors.

you get into these new stockers soon after they are planted in May, you'll be catching only small fish. If that happens, move to another area.

There are plenty of bugs in Dodge – caddisflies, mayflies, damsels galore, and all the rest. Fish it the way you would any of the impoundments. Because it is so big, it is one of the best spots during the hot summer period. You'll just need to fish early in the morning and late in the evening, when the trout are actively feeding.

Buckhorn Reservoir: About 5 miles along Marr Road from the intersection with Stage Road, Buckhorn is located in a small valley, and if you look back down the valley as you pass by, you can see the lake to your right (south). The dirt road is bumpy and rough, but it is only a mile to the reservoir, which generally offers excellent fishing. Buckhorn is planted with both Lahontan cutthroats and Eagle Lake

trout and is big enough so that it has a lot of holdovers. In the spring, fishing the weed beds and inlet at the upper end of the lake can be productive, but as the water level drops and the weather heats up, the fish tend to congregate in the deeper water near the dam. I've heard of fish up to thirteen or fourteen pounds being caught here, and although I haven't seen them, I believe it.

Round Corral Reservoir: Over the years, this impoundment has offered prime fishing, providing some real lunkers, although it covers only a few acres. Because of its small size and shallow depth, it is very dependent on precipitation, and winter kill can wipe out holdover trout. It can easily be fished with a float tube, or even from the bank.

The turnoff to Round Corral is off Marr Road a little less than 10 miles from the intersection with

Stage Road. There is no sign at the turnoff, which is to the left, but if you come to the Nevada border and see a lake beside the road, you've gone about 1.7 miles too far.

The rough dirt road to Round Corral (you can make it without four-wheel drive, but go slowly) is only a half a mile long – it tops a rise, then drops to the water, which is officially labeled "Round Corral Wetlands." If there have been a few wet years, enjoy fishing for lunkers. If not, well ... why not bring along your kids and let them catch some recently stocked trout?

Nelson Corral

Nelson Corral has pumped out some of the biggest fish in the area over the years. It used to be very difficult to get to, but the road has been improved a bit – although not as much as the springs and tires on your car would like. This is one of those reservoirs that the DFG biologists would love to see with a two-trout limit, but the locals won't hear of it. As a result, who knows whether it will have more than the current year's planters by the time you read this?

Use the little town of Likely, 19 miles south of Alturas on Highway 395, as a starting point. Likely is the home of the Most Likely Cafe and not much else. And how did Likely get its name? According to an old copy of Reader's Digest, city fathers some years back wanted to incorporate and offered several names, all of which were refused because they already existed elsewhere as towns.

One city father complained, "Are all the names taken?"

"Not likely," replied another. The vote for Likely was unanimous, although personally, I would have voted for Not Likely.

From Likely, go 7.5 miles south on Highway 395, almost to Sage Hen Summit. A dirt road turns off to the right (west) and ends in a T after only a hundred feet or so. Go left a few hundred yards to a green metal gate. Go through it (close it and all the others after you) and continue half a mile to a second green metal gate on your right. Go through it and up into the hills. At

an unmarked fork in the road, stay right and you'll come to yet another green metal gate. Not far beyond that third gate, the road forks, with the right branch going to the dam at Nelson Coral and the left to the shallow end of the reservoir. Both branches of the road are less than a mile long, but the road to the dam is miserable, with rocks, bumps, ruts, and all the rest of those things that give your internal organs a shakeup. The left-hand branch to the shallow end is much better.

It's actually only 4.1 miles from Highway 395 to the water, but it seems a lot farther. Nelson Corral is a good-sized reservoir, big enough to keep some very large trout alive, if they don't end up in somebody's freezer.

Smith Reservoir

This little reservoir is a quarter of a mile south on Highway 395, beyond the turnoff to Nelson Corral. It is right beside the highway, but is ignored by many anglers because they figure it is so easy to get to that everybody fishes it.

It is small enough so that a chance of catching a big trout is all but nonexistent. But you can have some fun casting from the dam and

pick up rainbows from twelve to fifteen inches stocked during the current year. It's a good place to take the kids and really is quite pretty, with occasional deer and antelope coming to the shore to drink.

The dirt road turnoff is to the left as you are going south and isn't easy to spot until you are right on it. If you can see the lake, you've gone too far. I use the shield-shaped Highway 395 markers on both sides of the road as my indicator – the turnoff is a few hundred feet south. There is a wire gate, and it is a hundred yards to the water.

Blue Lake and Clear Lake

Blue Lake and Clear Lake are in the South Warner Mountains, and each has something special to offer anglers. For Blue Lake, it is easy accessibility (paved road all the way) and the fact that it is one of the few natural stillwaters in Modoc County. For Clear Lake, it is wild trout, although you'll have to do a bit of hiking to get there. Both have much more of an alpine character than the desert reservoirs.

Access to these lakes is on Jess Valley Road (County Road 64), which turns east from Highway 395 at Likely. Blue Lake is 16 miles,

Bayley Reservoir is just plain ugly, but it does hold a lot of 13-16-inch trout.

The aptly-named Lily Lake is a pretty place to fish for stocked rainbows.

Clear Lake 15 miles. As the road enters Jess Valley, it splits, with the right fork going to Blue Lake and the left fork to Mill Creek Falls Campground, which is the starting point for the brief hike to Clear Lake.

Blue Lake has a good boat ramp, a 15-mile-per-hour speed limit for boats, and a large campground. It is a great spot for family camping and fishing. Stocked rainbows are the main fare, but it also holds some big browns that were stocked there years ago but have been able to reproduce in feeder streams. These browns aren't caught very often, but they are there.

Clear Lake is in the South Warner Wilderness, which borders the Mill Creek Falls Campground, and because of this is not stocked. The dirt trail to the lake starts from the campground parking lot and then forks, with the left branch going to the falls and the right branch to Clear Lake. It is only about a fifteen-minute walk, and if you don't want to haul along a float tube, it can be fished from the shore.

Bayley Reservoir

Bayley, less than 20 miles south of Alturas, is a sleeper, according to John King. He says that if they hit it at the right time, fly-line anglers can catch trout until their arm gets tired. Maybe not any of those ten-pounders, but plenty in the fourteen-to-sixteen-inch range.

That's the upside. The downside is that it isn't quite as scenic as Lake Tahoe.

To get there, take Highway 395 south from Alturas 6.3 miles and turn right (west) on Jones Lane (County Road 61). It dead-ends at County Road 60, where you turn left and parallel Highway 395 for a couple of miles before turning right on County Road 62. This gravel road will take you 3.5 miles to a fork, where a sign shows that Bayley Reservoir is 4 miles on the left-hand branch. The road isn't all that bad, at least compared with some of the others, but goes only to the dam – you can either walk or float tube to any other spots on the lake.

CEDARVILLE

To get to Cedarville, follow Highway 299/395 northeast from Alturas, then Highway 299 east to Cedarville, which is 23 miles from Alturas. County Road 1 goes north and south from Cedarville along the eastern slope of the Warner Mountains.

Sworinger Reservoir

This is one of the rare wild-trout lakes in this part of California – no stocking. That's the good news. The bad news is that there are no special restrictions on Sworinger, aside from a prohibition on fishing the

Sworinger is the only wild-trout reservoir in the Alturas area. Unfortunately, it has no special fishing regulations.

tributaries that are spawning areas for the wild rainbows.

It's a big lake sitting at almost 6,000 feet, and usually has plenty of water all year. There is limited access, because it is mostly on private land. There is a rough road to the upper, shallow portion of the lake and a little camping area with a toilet about a quarter-mile along the eastern side of the lake. The most popular area is the dam at the southern end. You have to go through a gate to get to the dam – don't forget to close it after you go through.

Near the dam is probably the best spot to fish, although rainbows are scattered throughout the lake. A favorite area is not far from the dam, where Silver Creek, the main tributary, runs into the reservoir.

Water clarity leaves something to be desired. Heavy algae growth makes seeing your fins difficult, but it doesn't seem to deter the fish.

There are a lot of them, including lunkers.

From Cedarville, go south on County Road 1 for 17 miles to Eagleville. The turnoff to Sworinger is to the west on County Road 42, 3 miles south of Eagleville. This is a washboard gravel road that winds steeply into the mountains. After about 4 miles, there is a fork – stay left on 42A, which a sign says goes to Lost Lake, but doesn't mention Sworinger. The reservoir is 3 miles on 42A.

Fee Reservoir

This has my vote as one of the ugliest reservoirs in the area, but locals insist it is the home of some big Lahontan cutthroats and can be productive even during the heat of summer. There isn't a tree within 100 miles, and its water generally is the color of mud.

To get there, follow County Road 1 north from Cedarville to the vil-

lage of Fort Bidwell. Just north of town there is a sign to Fee, which is another 8 miles along County Road 6. It is paved about halfway to the reservoir and then becomes good gravel as it goes into the hills. There is a campground, if you are so inclined.

HIGHWAY 395 NORTH

Highway 395/299 goes north from Alturas, with Highway 299 branching east to Cedarville 5 miles out of town and Highway 395 continuing north on the western flank of the Warner Mountains to Oregon.

There are several impoundments in the Warners that offer decent fishing for stocked trout and have more the character of alpine lakes than high-desert reservoirs.

Lily Lake and Cave Lake

Both lakes are on Forest Service Road 2, which turns east from

Highway 395 40 miles north of Alturas. Lily Lake is 5 miles and Cave Lake 6 miles on what is a fairly good gravel road that winds steeply uphill into the mountains. It isn't the place to tow along a travel trailer.

Both are small, only a couple of acres, and both have their names for a reason. Lily pads dot Lily Lake, offering shelter for stocked rainbows, while there is a cave that goes deep into a rock at Cave Lake. No camping is allowed at Lily, although it does have a picnic area with tables, along with a toilet. If you want to camp, Cave Lake is the place to go.

Briles Reservoir

Like Cave and Lily Lakes, this impoundment has Eagle Lake stockers. Its main recommendation is that the water is fairly clear, and it boasts a pretty, conifer-bordered shoreline. Another plus: It doesn't get nearly the pressure that Lily or Cave do.

There are numerous dead trees jutting from the lake, which offer good holding spots for trout. The top of one large tree that stretches forty feet into the air is the site for an osprey's nest most years. When she's there, mama osprey will look down on anglers and make angry noises, but won't leave her chicks unless she spots a fish that looks ripe for the taking.

Briles is big enough so there can be some decent-sized holdovers, but for the most part, you'll be catching ten-to-fourteen-inch rainbows.

To get to Briles, follow Highway 395 north about 20 miles to the town of Davis Creek, where you turn east on Forest Service Road 48 (it also is County Road 11). There are a number of forks in the road on the 8.5 mile drive to the lake, but if you stay left, you'll get to the right spot. There are plenty of signs, so you shouldn't lose your way. The last few hundred yards of the road are rutted and bumpy, so you'll have to go slowly.

HIGHWAY 299 WEST

A number of the reservoirs that at one time offered the best fishing in the area lie off Highway 299 west, toward Redding. Unfortunately, most of them no longer are worth the trip, unless you want to catch bass. Reservoirs C and F, part of the so-called Alphabet Reservoirs, were among the top fisheries, but tui chubs have taken over and pretty much eased trout out of the way, although there still are some rainbows. Reservoir C, in particular, now offers good fishing for largemouth bass.

Duncan Reservoir, in the same area, also had good trout fishing at one time, but now is for all practical purposes dead as far as fly-line anglers are concerned.

These reservoirs would be candidates for poisoning and restocking if the DFG had more freedom to use rotenone to kill unwanted fish.

Ballard Reservoir

Ballard is a fun place to fish, if you aren't looking for bigger trout. It is a fairly large reservoir in a wooded area, with flat spots to camp and not too much traffic. A word of caution: This reservoir is on private land, so keep it clean, or the rancher who owns it can decide to close it to the public.

To get to Ballard, go west on Highway 299 for 19 miles to the town of Canby. From Canby go left (south) on Centerville Road. Less than a

mile out of town, go right (actually straight, since Centerville Road turns left) on County Road 175. Follow this gravel road 1.5 miles to a fork, where a sign shows Ballard Reservoir to the left. There are other forks along the way, but if you stay to the left, you'll get to Ballard in another 5 miles.

Once you're at the reservoir, the left branch of the road goes to the dam, while the right fork follows the eastern shore, where flat areas good for camping are located. You can put in with a float tube just about anyplace. There is no designated boat ramp, although it is easy enough to launch a boat if it is small enough to do it by hand.

Chapter 6

Stone Lagoon, Big Lagoon

These two lagoons north of Eureka are undiscovered gems – undiscovered by just about everybody except a handful of locals. What they have to offer is unique: sea-run cutthroats and steelhead in two lovely lagoons separated from the ocean by a narrow sandbar.

A few times a year, when the heavy winter rains are pouring water into the lagoons and the ocean is running high, the sandbars break. This allows the cutthroats and steelhead to pass to and from the ocean. The sandbar may be open for a few days or a few weeks, but that is enough to keep the cycle moving.

The breach also allows salt water into the lagoons, creating the mixture of salt and fresh water called brackish water. Because salt water is heavier, it settles to the bottom in a defined layer, unless winds whip up the water enough to mix the two. Once the sandbar closes again, the inflow of fresh water from the feeder creeks makes the water progressively less brackish as the year wears on, although it does maintain some salt content. This is something to remember after you are through fishing – you'll need to clean your gear, and if you use a boat, flush the engine with fresh water.

Stone Lagoon is a part of the Department of Fish and Game's Catch-and-Release Program. Anglers must use barbless hooks, and no bait is allowed. Two cutthroats fourteen inches or longer can be kept, but all other salmonids, including steelhead, must be released.

Stone Lagoon can be fished either from shore or with a boat or float tube. Mike Kuczynski uses a canoe to get to where he wants to wade.

Sea-run cutthroat show very little of the red gill slash that earned cutthroat their name.

McDonald Creek flows into Stone Lagoon at the south end and is a spawning area for the cutthroats and steelhead. Because they use the same area to spawn, many of the fish, particularly the cutthroats, are hybrids. Most of the cutthroats are silver-colored, almost like steelhead. Occasionally, they will have a bit of the distinctive red slash under their gills that gives the cutthroat its name, but this is not always the case.

There are four lagoons that stretch along Highway 101 in this area. To the north of Stone Lagoon, on the east side of the highway, is Freshwater Lagoon. It does not break open to the ocean and is stocked with hatchery rainbows and bass.

Big Lagoon is to the south. Regulations are the same as on Stone Lagoon, except that the keeper size limit for cutthroat is ten inches or longer.

There also is an area called Dry Lagoon, which is a marsh, rather than a lagoon, and has no fishing. It is between Big Lagoon and Stone Lagoon.

The lagoons are 35 miles north of Eureka on Highway 101, and except for Freshwater Lagoon, are part of the Humboldt Lagoons State Park. Big, Stone, and Freshwater Lagoons have boat ramps. There also is a visitor's center at Stone Lagoon. Across the lagoon from the visitor's center, in an area called Ryan's Cove, there are six camping spots accessible only by boat. Otherwise, there is camping just to the south at Patrick's Point Park or a few miles north at the town of Orrick.

No matter which of the lagoons you are fishing, you need to be aware of the weather. The wind can come up suddenly and be vicious – don't forget that only a bit of sand separates the lagoons from the open ocean. Float tubers who are a long way from their put-in can get into trouble trying to make their way home against a strong blow.

Stone Lagoon, separated from the ocean by a narrow spit of sand, has sea-run cutthroat and steelhead.

This is not an easy body of water to fish. Galen Petty, a Eureka fly-line angler who has been fishing Stone Lagoon for more than three decades, says,

"No matter how much you fish Stone Lagoon, it takes persistence and good presentation. Know that you're going to spend a bit of time on the water to figure it out, but if you cover it well and find fish, the fishing can be fantastic."

STONE LAGOON

This is not an easy body of water to fish. Galen Petty, a Eureka fly-line angler who has been fishing Stone Lagoon for more than three decades, says, "No matter how much you fish Stone Lagoon, it takes persistence and good presentation. Know that you're going to spend a bit of time on the water to figure it out, but if you cover it well and find fish, the fishing can be fantastic."

He fishes the water differently when it is high or low. When high, the lagoon spreads over the banks and into surrounding grassy areas, which in effect become weed beds. When that happens, Petty fishes along the edges of the grass. When the water is low, he stalks trout along the shore, fishing drop-offs and other structure or casting to fish that are in the shallows.

Although fish can be scattered throughout the 521-acre lake, there are several places that are the hot spots. When the water is low, one of these is the mile-long sandbar separating the lagoon from the ocean. It is a shallow area where an angler can walk out a hundred feet or so and look for fish cruising in a couple of feet of water or throw flies over the drop-off, which is clearly visible, and let them sink.

The sand spit is accessible from a paved road west off Highway 101 at the northern end of the lake. It is clearly marked with a sign. There is a portable toilet, parking, and a place to launch a small boat. Anglers can fish along the spit, wading out into the shallow water and casting to likely areas.

Another spot that usually produces fish is Ryan's Cove, which also is on the western shore. You can get there by walking along the sandbar, or it is accessible by boat or float tube. Cutthroats tend to hang out in the cove, which is easily recognizable because it is the only well-defined cove on the lagoon. The cuts can be any size from eight to twenty-six inches, but most of them are in the twelve-to-eighteen-inch range.

Petty suggests streamer patterns in about a size 8. He uses leeches, Woolly Buggers, and bait imitations in browns, greens, blacks, and whites. Mohair Leeches and Muddler Minnows in those colors work well, as does a Sparkle Bugger.

Along the southeastern shore, nymphs seem to draw more strikes. The standard fare – Zug Bugs, PTs, Bird's Nests, and Prince Nymphs, size 12 and 14 – are the flies of choice.

Another common food in the lagoon is scuds. They are rust or olive in color and are about a size 14.

BIG LAGOON

Big Lagoon offers almost as good fishing, but is even more demanding. There is a boat ramp at the southern end of the 1,470-acre lagoon, and, as at Stone Lagoon, walking along the 3.2-mile sandbar separating the ocean from the lagoon can be an effective way to fish. Again, the sandbar separating the lagoon from the ocean is easy to reach – it

begins at the southern end of Big Lagoon, where the boat ramp, picnic area, toilets, and parking lot are located.

Big Lagoon is more likely to break open to the ocean several times during the stormy winter months, with more fish coming in and out. Right after such a break is a good time to be on the water, with the newly entered fish providing hot angling.

There are cutthroats, which tend to be smaller than in Stone Lagoon, but there also are larger steelhead. They run about eight pounds, and Petty has caught a thirteen-pounder. Silver salmon regularly make their way into the lagoon, too, and if hooked provide excellent sport. Just remember that all steelhead and salmon have to be immediately released.

Petty says that in the fall and winter, the best bet is to fish the northern end, looking for cruising fish. During other times of the year, the cutts often hang out at the southwestern end of the lagoon.

Another good spot is at the mouth of Maple Creek, which flows in at the southeastern corner. The creek is on private property, so you can't fish it from the bank. Even if you have a boat or float tube, the water above the second bridge on Maple Creek is private. If you stray into private water, a guard is likely to cite you for trespassing.

FRESHWATER LAGOON

There's nothing the matter with fishing Freshwater Lagoon – it just doesn't have the sea-run cutthroats and steelhead that make Stone Lagoon and Big Lagoon unique. It is regularly stocked with rainbows and bass, and there are a lot of large holdover bass.

There are boat ramps at both ends of the lagoon, which is sixteen feet deep at its deepest point.

The best fishing is at the south end of the lagoon, where the bigger rainbows and bass tend to congregate. Lily pads in this area offer protection to the bass and make for fun fishing with poppers. There are no special regulations on Freshwater Lagoon.

Resources

The only fly shop in this area is the **Eureka Fly Shop**, 1632 Broadway, Eureka, CA 95501. The phone is (707) 444-2000. It has up-to-date information along with a wide range of fly-fishing gear.

For information about lodging and other attractions in the area, call or write the **Humboldt County Convention and Visitor's Bureau**, 1034 Second Street, Eureka, CA 95501, telephone (800) 346-3482. Their web site is www.redwoodvisitor.org, and they can be reached by e-mail at redwoodvis@aol.com.

For information on the **Humboldt Lagoons State Park**, call the park office at (707) 488-2041 or write them at 15336 Highway 101, Trinidad, CA 95570.

Stone Lagoon

Restoration of a native trout habitat

Stone Lagoon has had its ups and downs over the years, but always seems to rebound from problems because of its rich supply of food.

The California Department of Fish and Game for years used Stone Lagoon and Big Lagoon as dumping grounds for hatchery-raised fish. They were easily accessible, and if for some reason fish could not be planted in their scheduled waters, they went into the lagoons. Silver and king salmon, steelhead, and rainbows were put into the lagoons until the mid-1980s, when the wild-trout ethic began to gather steam. CalTrout and other angling groups pushed the DFG to make Stone lagoon a native fishery by planting only the sea-run cutthroats that inhabit some of Northern California's coastal waters.

A number of volunteer organizations contributed to restoration work on feeder streams to improve spawning habitat. The bulk of the work was on McDonald Creek, which feeds Stone Lagoon at the southern end. With the help of Humboldt State University in nearby Arcata, a handful of native sea-run cutthroat were trapped from several North Coast streams, then spawned at the university, and the fry were planted in Stone Lagoon to propagate and provide a population of wild fish.

Things went along well for a some years, with the fishery steadily improving. But then came several major setbacks. During the summer of 1993, an unidentified person illegally opened Stone Lagoon to the ocean. The result was that the lagoon, which is slightly above sea level, all but emptied. In the winter, when the lagoons breech naturally, there is fresh water pouring in from rain, which maintains the water level. In the summer, when the artificial breech was created, there was no incoming water, so the level dropped drastically, and most of the fish were killed or dispersed into the ocean.

Restocking helped restore the balance, but the January 1997 floods that occurred throughout Northern California wiped out much of the work that had restored the spawning areas in McDonald Creek. There are no definite plans to repair the damage.

Then there is the problem of the tidewater goby, an inch-long, bottom feeding fish that lives in brackish water. Studies done during the drought years in the late 1980s showed that the goby was disappearing. As a result, it was put on the Interim Endangered Species List in 1994, and since 1996 that has prevented the DFG from planting cutthroats because the goby is just the right size to make a tasty morsel for the cutts.

In fact, later studies showed that once the drought was over, there were plenty of tidewater gobies around, and the federal agency promised to get it delisted. But the delisting got sidetracked – the feds didn't provide adequate time for public comment. When the action will be taken is anybody's guess, but until it is, there will be no more cutthroats planted in the lagoon.

Stone Lagoon is separated from the ocean by only a narrow strip of sand, as seen on the far right.

Chapter 7

Lewiston Lake
and Grass Valley Creek Reservoir

Lewiston Lake and Grass Valley Creek Reservoir offer two different types of still-water fly fishing. Lewiston, the afterbay of Trinity Lake, is a tailwater fishery with cold, clear water that moves steadily through the narrow reservoir. Grass Valley Creek Reservoir is a hike-in lake that holds landlocked steelhead.

Of the two, Lewiston Lake has the best fishing. There is something for everybody – ten-to-fourteen-inch stocked rainbows for eat-'em anglers, along with some big and feisty holdovers and a few wild trout for those who want to test their fly-fishing skills. It's not easy going, particularly fishing the minuscule midges that the big trout love to sip.

While this chapter centers on these two bodies of water, Trinity Lake (officially known as Clair Engle Reservoir, but nobody calls it that) also deserves a mention. The third-largest reservoir in California, it is loaded with fish. But for the fly-line angler, the fishing is good only at certain places and times. Most of the year, trout hold deep enough so that bait-and-lure anglers do better, particularly by trolling.

If you want to fish Trinity Lake, the spring and fall are the best seasons. During the summer, the trout (and bass and kokanee) hold deeper, making them tougher to get on a fly line, and in the winter, it is just too cold.

Concentrate on the feeder inlets, particularly in the spring. Specifically, the Upper Trinity / Coffee Creek inlet and the East Fork Trinity inlet, both at the northern end of the lake, and Swift Creek and the Stuart Fork on the western side.

Joe Neil sets up on a rainbow that sipped a midge nymph fished just under the surface on Lewiston Lake.

LEWISTON LAKE

Like many of California's better trout stillwaters, Lewiston isn't still – it has enough current so that at times it fishes more like a spring creek than a dammed-up reservoir.

Lewiston is used to control the flow of water into the Trinity River and through the Carr Powerhouse into Whiskeytown Lake, near Redding, with about 3,500 cubic feet of water flowing out of Lewiston each second. The input from Trinity Lake is much more variable, because it depends on the demand for electricity, but it can be enough to raise the lake level sharply. In any case, there usually is enough water coming in and going out to maintain a steady movement along the narrow, 6-mile lake. The water from Trinity comes from deep in the reservoir, maintaining about

a 50-degree temperature year around, and there is the added bonus of a 10-mile-per-hour speed limit for boats, which keeps the jet skis and water-skiers out of your hair. What this adds up to is perfect trout water.

To get to Lewiston Lake, take Highway 299 west from Redding 30 miles over Buckhorn Summit, then turn north on Road 105 to the town of Lewiston. From Lewiston, Trinity Dam Boulevard parallels the western side of the lake, offering access to campgrounds, launch ramps, and other facilities.

There's pretty much something for everybody in Lewiston Lake. For novices, stocked rainbows and a plentiful supply of kokanee (a type of landlocked salmon) are relatively easy to catch. For the more advanced fly-line angler, big rain-

bows, browns, and even brookies cruise the lake, sipping midges or slashing at emerging mayflies and caddises.

It isn't easy fishing for the big ones – Lewiston's water is clear, and the trout, which often can be found in shallow areas, are extremely spooky. To get these lunkers, you need to stalk them and be able to handle long leaders and long, soft casts.

There are mud flats on both sides of the lake about two-thirds of the way down, across from Lakeview Terrace Resort, where some big trout gather in channels, then move onto flats only a foot or two deep to feed. These flats are difficult to fish from a float tube because they aren't deep enough for an angler in a belly boat to move without stirring up the mud. This is

Joe Neil works a slot on Lewiston Lake, looking for a big rainbow.

Tips from Joe Neil for Fishing Lewiston Lake

■ To catch big trout, you need to be wary. Try to spot a working fish and cast to it. Don't just blind cast, or you'll put down every fish in the area.

■ Bigger holdover fish sometimes cruise on the edges of pods of smaller, more recent planters. So when looking for large trout, don't ignore groups of smaller fish.

■ You have to stalk fish that are cruising. Watch what they are doing and cast to where you think they will be on the next rise. You must be able to cast fifty feet and lay a dry fly down without a rip-

ple. Long leaders in the 12-foot range are necessary, but you can use 4X tippets, particularly if they are made of the less visible fluorocarbon.

■ When fishing midges, just let them sit, or move them so slowly that it is agonizing. If a fish is nearby, sometimes a very slight twitch can get its attention.

■ At the two islands just south of the boat launch at Pine Cove Marina, there almost always are fish working in the current that flows between them. But there is room for only one person to fish this area at a time.

a case where a pontoon boat that keeps most of your body out of the water is a better bet.

The flats on the west shore can be fished by wading. Park your car along the road near Lakeview Terrace and work your way through the weeds. There generally are some beaten-down areas where others have forced their way through the growth. Be careful wading – it can be muddy.

If the water is moving, as it usually is, cast out into the current and let your fly drift, just as if you were fishing a spring creek. This is a great area if there is a hatch and you can float a dry fly in the current.

For those who want to tube the flats, there are several places to get into the water, including a easy-launch area just south of Lakeview Terrace. North of the resort, there is a dirt road paralleling the main road that also offers launching access.

Joe Neil, a long-time fly fisherman and retired guide who lives on the shores of Lewiston Lake, suggests that in fishing the lake, anglers should "look for surface activity or go to a known hold and present accordingly – nymphs until the duns show, then switch to dries for the mayfly action. Size 12 through 18 PTs or Hare's Ears work well for the *Callibaetis*. Sparkle Duns will get a rise, as well as Quigley Cripples in size 14 to 18. Some of the *Callibaetis* can grow quite large, to size 12, and they come in two colors, olive dun and a dark orange.

"Try size 14 to 18 Bird's Nests for the small caddises and size 8 through 12 orange-brown nymphs for the October Caddis hatch. An Elk Hair or X-Caddis, size 14 to 20, can work well in the evening after the sun leaves the water. Black Woolly Buggers are a favorite most of the time, and scuds will get a pull, too."

And then there are the midges. Neil says, "Midges, size 18 to 26, are the most prolific insects in Lewiston. Their shucks can leave a layer of flotsam on the surface that can look downright unhealthy at times. They will hatch every day of the year, in the morning, midday, in the evening, and I suspect at night. When the fish are actively taking midges, which is normally when there is little or no wind, a size 18 to 22 suspender midge [a midge pattern that will sit in the film] with the same size pupa in tandem about six to eight inches below is the surest way to get a hit, since most of the action takes place close to the film.

"Midges move agonizingly slowly, so any movement must be barely perceptible or not at all. Pods of fish will cruise the surface, sipping emergers, and will spook if your cast lands too close. So use a long leader."

Neil has another tip while fishing this way – one most of us wouldn't think about. "If you're right-handed and fishing from a tube or pontoon boat, try and keep the working pod on your left, circling them clockwise. This will allow you to keep the fish in sight and still cast accurately across your body. Left-handers do the opposite."

Another good area is around the two islands near the launch ramp at Pine Cove Marina. Jim Deichler, owner of the marina, has built a handy float-tube put-in that is free. And for a small fee, you can put in at Pine Cove and float to Lakeview Terrace, where he will pick you up at an appointed time with a shuttle.

Deichler also has started his own fish-stocking program for the lake, raising pens of rainbows and brookies at his dock until they are several pounds each and then turning them loose in Lewiston. He finances the program with barbeques, donations, and some help from the local chamber of commerce.

Fishing at the upper end of Lewiston, near where water comes out from Trinity Lake, can be done with a boat, float tube, or by wading. But … when they decide to step up the power supply, the water flow will pick up suddenly, and the water level can rise a foot or more within minutes. Just remember this if you decide to go wading – don't get cut off from high ground.

Although there is supposed to be a warning siren whenever increased water flow is planned, Neil says it is almost never sounded.

GRASS VALLEY CREEK RESERVOIR

First the bad news. This is a walk-in lake, and that means tough going if you are carrying a float tube and all the accompanying gear. Not that it is a long way (1.7 miles) or that the trail is bad (it's a road), but it involves some up-and-down slogging, with two high ridges to cross. Coming out is particularly difficult because of a long, uphill stretch coming up from the lake.

The good news is that this reservoir can provide fun fishing for land-locked steelhead, plus an occasional brown – and they are nowhere near as demanding of the fly-line angler as the educated, spooky lunkers at Lewiston Lake. The fish are wild, trapped there when the reservoir was built in 1990 to catch the silt washed down from upstream. The creek below the dam is undergoing restoration, and sedimentation was one of its major problems.

Grass Valley Creek Reservoir is designated as catch-and-release water, which in this case means it has a two-fish limit and that only barbless lures and flies can be used. It is open to fishing all year, but this area can be cold and snowy, so fishing it in the winter when the trout are sluggish isn't really an option.

The parking area to walk into the reservoir is a small pullout on the southern side of Highway 299 just west of Buckhorn Summit, about 25 miles from Redding. Going west on 299, there is a large brown-and-white sign that says "Grass Valley Creek Watershed." On the opposite side of the highway is a paved road with a gated entrance. This actually is the road to the reservoir, but it is on private land, and no parking or walking on this section of the road is allowed. The unpaved parking area that anglers must use is about a hundred yards east toward Buckhorn Summit on 299, an unmarked pullout with room for several cars. From the pull-out, a steep, primitive trail leads downhill through a fence and to the road, which can be used from here on. There's some talk of improving this short trail, but nothing definite is in the works.

Grass Valley Creek Reservoir is a pretty, hike-in lake offering fine fishing for landlocked steelhead.

If you are coming from the west on Highway 299, there is a small brown-and-white sign just before the two turnouts that says "Shingle Shanty."

Once an angler is down the trail and on the road, it soon forks, with the right branch going to the Grass Valley Creek Reservoir dam and the left fork leading to the inlet where the creek comes in. If you head toward the inlet, there is another fork after 1.2 miles. Go to the right downhill along an unsurfaced road (the left fork is gravel and goes up) to where it dead-ends at the creek inlet. When you are walking in, keep an eye out for rattlesnakes, bears, and even an occasional elk from a herd that holds in the area.

This is private land, but the owner does not live in the area and has not put up gates, signs, or structures. Local officials say there are no restrictions to using the inlet area for fishing, but anglers should, as always, leave it cleaner than they found it.

The reservoir itself is deep and narrow, covering about forty-five surface acres. It is quite pretty, with heavily wooded banks and plenty of aquatic weed growth. Since it is used to catch sediment, rather than for irrigation or power, it usually is full, without the water fluctuations that can leave those ugly "bathtub rings" around some reservoirs.

About halfway between the inlet and dam, near a point where the reservoir bends, there is a wooded island with weeds along the bank. This is an excellent area for dry-fly fishing when there is a mayfly or caddis hatch. A second island closer to the dam also can be productive.

There are damselflies, dragonflies, and midges, and any of the standard imitations will work just fine. The midge hatch here is not nearly as heavy as it is on Lewiston Lake.

For the most part, anglers will be catching steelhead up to fourteen or fifteen inches, but there are larger ones in the lake. The trouble is, they become wary and usually don't fall prey to an artificial lure. As with most such lakes, fishing it in the spring is the best, with fall as a runner-up. Summer is slow, with the trout holding deeper, unless you are there about dusk, when there may be brief, but heavy surface action.

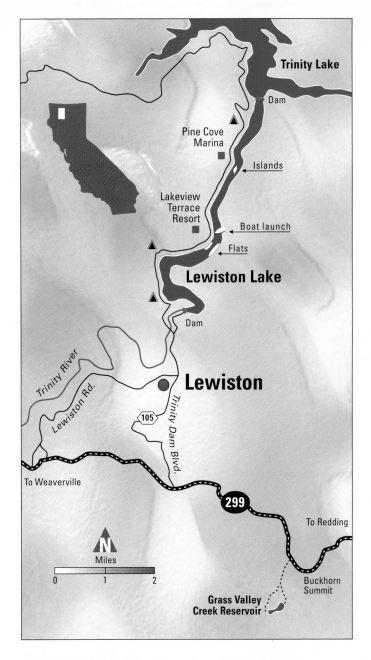

Resources

The only full-service fly shop in this area is the **Trinity Fly Shop**, on Lewiston Road, 4.5 miles outside the town of Lewiston. The telephone is (530) 623-6757, their web site is www.trinityflyshop.com, and e-mail is trinflyguy@tcoe.trinity.k12.ca.us.

The **Trinity County Chamber of Commerce** offers details for camping and just about anything else you need to know about the area. It can be reached at (800) 421-7259 or www.trinitycountry.com. The address is 211 Trinity Lake Boulevard, Weaverville, CA 96093.

For information on **U.S. Forest Service campgrounds** in the Trinity/Lewiston Lakes area, call the Weaverville Ranger Station at (530) 623-2121. Their address is 210 Main Street, Highway 299, Weaverville, CA 96093.

Chapter 8

The Redding area

MANZANITA McCUMBER IRON CANYON ORR
JUANITA CASTLE GUMBOOT BULLSEYE

Northern California to the north and east of Redding offers some of the best trout fishing in the state. The rivers are so good – the upper Sacramento, McCloud, Pit, and Fall Rivers, to name the blue-ribbon best – that lakes and reservoirs go almost unnoticed by many fly-line anglers.

That's a big mistake, folks. There are large trout, and plenty of them, in a variety of impoundments within easy striking distance. Apart from Manzanita Lake, which is a wild-trout fishery, most of the rest contain stocked rainbows, along with holdovers and a few wild trout, including browns. In some waters, browns and brookies also are planted.

Awe-inspiring scenery is abundant, and so

are some great small towns that are geared to fishing. Although this chapter is entitled "The Redding Area," that's just a starting point. Forty-five minutes north of Redding on Interstate 5 is Dunsmuir, which has become the quintessential little fishing town. Then, to the east, there are McCloud and Burney, which see thousands of anglers every year, many of them fly-line types.

Dunsmuir remains my favorite, a strip town that shares a canyon with the beautiful upper Sacramento River and two of Northern California's busiest byways – Interstate 5 and the Southern Pacific Railroad. Dunsmuir was a railway town and still has a big train station and even a railroad museum, but its main industry now is catering to visitors who come for the fishing. There are plenty of places to stay in Dunsmuir, along with a couple of excellent restaurants. There also are two full-service fly shops, which isn't bad for a town that counts only 2,000 inhabitants.

For some, the only downside to staying in Dunsmuir is the regular moan of railway-engine whistles and the rumble of long freight trains passing through day and night. Personally, I enjoy the sound. It reminds me not only of growing up in Idaho, but of the fact that the Southern Pacific Railway tracks are a crucial pathway for anglers walking along the upper Sacramento River.

A typical Manzanita Lake brown. There are plenty of them but they are tough to catch.

Richard Burns casts to rising fish on Manzanita Lake in Lassen Volcanic National Park. Manzanita is a prime spot for fly-line anglers.

Of course, when you mention stillwaters in the Redding area, the largest body of water in California, Shasta Lake, comes to mind (only half of Lake Tahoe is in California). Although there are plenty of trout in this huge lake, it just isn't a fly-fisher's dream. It can be fun if you have a boat and can motor deep into one of the arms in the spring or fall, when the fish are in shallower water. This is particularly true of the Pit River arm, where the top section flows as a river when the water is low. However, since it is considered part of the lake, it is open to fishing year-round.

Another plus for the Pit River arm is that it never was logged prior to building the dam, as were the three other Shasta Lake arms. As a

result, it has more structure on the bottom and is better for fishing for both trout and bass.

For the most part, however, Shasta Lake ranks higher as a lure-and-bait bass fishery than for trout, so I'll just offer this for-the-record passing mention, lest you think I've totally ignored it.

Stillwater fisheries in this chapter are scattered across a wide area. On the assumption that many anglers are arriving on I-5, directions on how to get to the various lakes and reservoirs will start from Redding or one of the major towns on the interstate north of Redding. The lakes good enough to rate detailed instructions are Manzanita, McCumber, Iron Canyon, Orr, and Juanita, with others mentioned as also-rans.

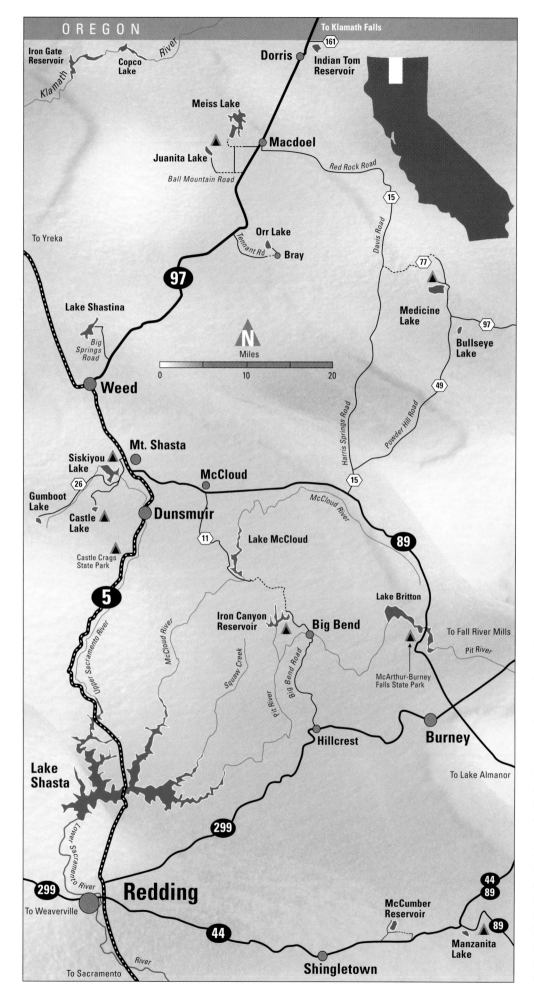

MANZANITA LAKE

This catch-and-release lake is in Lassen Volcanic National Park and offers a supply of wild rainbow and brown trout that draws anglers from all over California. Because it is in the park, anglers have to pay the regular admission fee to get there, just like everybody else.

There is a big campground (179 spots) and an unimproved boat ramp. Only boats without motors are allowed. At fifty-three surface acres, it is small enough to be handled easily with a float tube, although you may spend as much time gazing at the awesome scenery as at your fly line.

Both rainbows and browns are able to spawn in the creeks that feed Manzanita. And they live well, due to the abundant amount of available food. There are scuds, leeches, snails, damselflies, and dragonflies, not to mention terrestrials such as beetles and grasshoppers. And of course, mayflies and caddisflies also are plentiful.

With all this food, Manzanita is a match-the-hatch lake. In other words, it's a tough place for novice fly-line anglers. If you get too frustrated, Reflection Lake, just across the road, is stocked, has no special restrictions, and can provide fun family fishing.

Ice-out is a good time to fish Manzanita – if you can get in. Nobody is allowed into the park until the road is cleared of snow and the gates to the park are opened. The good news is that the Manzanita entrance usually is opened early in the spring, since it is on Highway 89.

During the period just after the ice breaks up, the fish are hungry and not very selective. Give them something big and juicy to eat such as a Woolly Bugger with a bit of flash on it to make it even more noticeable. As spring and summer wear on, the fishing becomes more difficult, and longer leaders, 12 or 14 feet, become necessary.

Terry Edelmann, a fly tier from Redding, likes to fish beetle imitations during the summer and recommends a fuzzy foam beetle that will rest on the surface for a while and then slowly sink. His favorite spot on the small lake is where Manzanita Creek enters the lake near the entrance shack – not far from where visitors leave their vehicles. Debris piles up at the creek

McCumber Reservoir often is overlooked by fly fishers. A big mistake, particularly in summer when the water is down.

mouth, and big fish hang around that area to take advantage of both the food washing in and the protection from the debris.

His recommended flies for Manzanita are Pheasant Tail or Flashback Pheasant Tail Nymphs or a Baum Lake Special, which is tied with a peacock herl body and a soft hackle.

To get to Manzanita, take Highway 44 from Redding 48 miles, then turn south about a mile on Highway 89 and go through the park entrance, where you pay. Manzanita is just off the highway.

McCUMBER RESERVOIR

McCumber Reservoir is so close to the more famous Manzanita Lake that it often is overlooked by fly fishers. Although McCumber doesn't have the catch-and-release designation that Manzanita has, it is an excellent fishery.

The lake was created by damming the north fork of Battle Creek and is used by Pacific Gas & Electric for hydroelectric power. No gas motors are allowed on the lake, but electric motors are permitted. The Department of Fish and Game stocks it with catchable trout, and there are plenty of larger holdovers, plus a population of wild trout that spawn in the creek.

The only real secret to fishing McCumber is that when it is low, go to the old creek channel, where the fish hold in deeper, cooler water. This channel winds along the eastern side of the lake, rather than down the middle. When full, McCumber covers 127 surface acres and has a maximum depth of nineteen feet, but when low, it gets down to about twenty-five acres and is only about seven feet deep.

During the winter, the action is mostly on midges and small *Callibaetis* mayflies. In the spring and summer, there is more of a choice, with larger *Callibaetis*, a variety of caddisflies, damselflies, and a large number of dragonflies. Dragonfly nymph imitations are an excellent choice to catch big fish in May and into June.

In the summer, heavy algae growth can make fishing difficult. In addition, it's so hot during midsummer that McCumber probably isn't the best place to be.

Fishing picks up again in the fall, when the browns become aggressive. Subsurface flies are best then, including minnows, leech imitations, and Woolly Worms.

There are trout ranging to eight pounds in McCumber, including plenty in the two-to-three-pound range and numerous ten-inchers and twelve-inchers, a lot of them wild fish. If an angler wants to catch a lot of fish, most of them planters, the place to go is near the dam.

I had a day on McCumber that offered a rare, unexpected treat – stalking fish on mud flats on the western edge of the lake. The day was sunny, the water was clear, the mud flats along the shore were pretty much barren of weed growth, and the fish had absolutely no right to be in a foot or two of water. Yet there they were, rainbows of twelve and fourteen inches, cruising singly or in pairs.

The trick was to cast a nymph a couple of feet in front of them without spooking them, let it settle to the bottom, then give it a twitch as they approached. This technique was absolutely deadly, and as much fun as trout fishing gets.

To get to McCumber, take Highway 44 east from Redding for 36 miles, then turn north on Lake McCumber Road. It is 1.7 miles to the reservoir. There is a small, primitive campground at the dam, but the launch ramp is about half a mile along Ritts Mill Road, which turns off to the west.

IRON CANYON RESERVOIR

For those of you who suffer from cabin fever in the late winter or early spring and are looking for a place to fish, this can be the spot. When many other reservoirs are filling up with cloudy water due to snowmelt, Iron Canyon stays low and clear. The reason is that it gets most of its water from Lake McCloud by way of a huge underground pipe. Then the water is run through turbines to produce electricity, flows into Iron Canyon Creek, and

eventually empties into the Pit River. Not until early summer is enough water released into this reservoir to fill it up. When full, it is less productive for the fly fisher – leave it to the Power Bait set.

To get there, take Highway 299 east from Redding. After 38 miles, turn north on Big Bend Road and then go 22 miles to the reservoir. The last 5 miles of the road, from the little village of Big Bend, are riddled with potholes, so drive slowly enough to save your car's wheel alignment. At the lake, the road turns to gravel and makes an 11-mile circuit around the shore, with dirt logging roads allowing access to the water.

There are two campgrounds, Hawkins Landing, which has a boat ramp, and Deadlun Creek. Camping is primitive, with no potable water, and there isn't room for large RVs or trailers.

Iron Canyon Reservoir sits at 2,700 feet in the Shasta-Trinity National Forest. Its 500 surface acres have an unusual configuration – a fairly small main lake behind the dam at the southern end, with most of the water concentrated in five arms, which gives an angler plenty of shoreline to fish. Each of the arms is fed by a creek, and those are the best places to fish, because the fish, including some big browns, are concentrated near the mouths of inlets,

along with the area called "The Tube," where the water from Lake McCloud comes in.

Terry Edelmann, who fishes Iron Canyon regularly during the winter and early spring, says, "Fish it when it is down, when the fish pile up at the mouths of the creeks. There are very few people who come to Iron Canyon during that winter / early spring period. They don't realize how good it can be. I find it more productive than [Lake] McCloud." Edelmann suggests using a dark Woolly Bugger or a bright-hued sunfish pattern – light olives, oranges, and yellows, blended with Krystal Flash. A San Juan worm can be deadly when there is a midge hatch.

And there are an incredible number of midges at McCumber. Edelmann says that when he walks in the mud along the bank, there sometimes are so many in the goo that the mud on his shoes is almost red.

The road to Iron Canyon splits when it reaches a summit overlooking the lake. You can go either way, because it encircles the reservoir. If you turn right, you cross the five creeks that feed the reservoir – McGill Creek, Deadlun Creek, Cedar Salt Log Creek, a small creek that has no name on maps, but flows all year, and Gap Creek. There are logging roads that allow some access to the mouths of all of these creeks, although in some places it is easier to leave your vehicle on the road and pick your way through the trees to the shore. A small boat is effective at Iron Canyon because it allows access to several creek mouths. Otherwise, try fishing it from the bank or use a float tube to get into position to cast into the moving water as it comes into the lake.

To get to the other top place to find fish, The Tube, you take an unmarked dirt road leading to the shoreline 4.7 miles from where the road from Big Bend reaches Iron Canyon. The road is only a couple of hundred yards long, but requires a four-wheel-drive vehicle. If it is wet, don't try it, even with a 4x4, because the red clay of the area becomes ice-slick and you might not be able to make it back up. In any case, it's a short walk from the road.

Once you reach the shore, there is no doubt where The Tube is located. The water roars as it boils up, setting

Terry Edelmann shows why fly fishing McCumber Reservoir is worthwhile.

Terry Edelmann works the moving water coming out of The Tube area of Iron Canyon Reservoir.

up a strong current that flows along this arm of the reservoir. Drifting big Woolly Buggers through this current will catch sizable trout. There are a couple of places on the bank where casting to the edge of the maelstrom is possible. If you have a boat, put yourself in the moving water and let the current do the work, fishing along the way. Once the drift stops, row or motor back and do it again.

Float tubes or pontoon boats can be used, but it is tough going. To begin with, the turbulence where the water comes up is strong enough to be dangerous, so you need to stay well away from the boil. In addition, the current moves right along, so holding in one spot is difficult, and there are back eddies that make kicking very tiring. All in all, I'd recommend using your float tube or pontoon boat somewhere else.

Although the main catch, particularly in the spring, is rainbows, there are a lot of big browns in Iron Canyon.

They come to the creeks to spawn in the fall, so a visit then also can be worthwhile.

Edelmann also suggests that anglers keep an eye out for a cranefly hatch and fish larva imitations if you spot one. A cranefly larva looks like a grub or a fat caddis larva. Edelmann says a good imitation is a blond Woolly Worm, size 10, tied on a 2X-long hook with light tan or cream dubbing. "Fish under an indicator, but try to get it just off the bottom, then give it a strip every once in a while, because they burrow into the mud, then rise to the surface to hatch," he says.

A quick word about Lake McCloud, which feeds Iron Canyon. It can be reached from the town of McCloud on Squaw Valley Road, a 10-mile drive to the south. It's a beautiful lake, and the McCloud River, which runs into and out of the lake, is one of California's best rivers for trout fishing. Although there are plenty of trout in the lake,

because it has steep banks and is deep, it is not very productive for fly fishers. Better to try Iron Canyon or one of the other lakes in the area.

ORR LAKE AND JUANITA LAKE

There is a string of lakes off Highway 97 stretching from the town of Weed, on Interstate 5, 68 miles north of Redding, all the way to the Oregon border. Only a couple offer good fly fishing – Orr and Juanita Lakes.

First, let's dispense with the other lakes. Lake Shastina, just north of Weed, is the largest and most easily accessible of the local stillwaters, but it's not much good for fly fishing except for bass in the spring. Otherwise, it is Power Bait and worm country. Meiss Lake, near the town of Macdoel, is part of the Butte Valley Wildlife Area, and although a great place for bird-watching, it is shallow

Christina Jones releases an Iron Canyon Reservoir rainbow caught from the bank on a midge pattern.

and pretty much barren of fish. Indian Tom Lake, northeast of the town of Dorris, holds cutthroat trout, but it is stagnant, with lots of weeds. You need to cover water to get fish, which is better done with spinning gear than a fly rod.

Orr and Juanita Lakes are off Highway 97 between Weed and Macdoel and are very similar in the way they fish. The big difference is that Juanita, which is at 5,100 feet elevation and covers fifty surface acres, is more developed, with camping spots, a good launch ramp, and other amenities. Orr, 500 feet lower and twice the size, is reached via a bumpy, rutted dirt road and offers only primitive camping, a gravel launch ramp, and a small dock. Both lakes are quite shallow – Juanita has a maximum depth of fifteen feet, while Orr's deepest area is only eleven feet. Both become considerably shallower in the summer, when

water is taken out.

To get to Orr, follow Highway 97 for 28 miles northeast from Weed, then turn east on Tennant Road and go 5 miles to Old State Highway, which takes you 2 more miles to the village of Bray, a cluster of half a dozen houses. As you enter Bray, the road turns from gravel to pavement, and there is an unmarked turnoff to the left (north) that crosses first the railway tracks, then a creek, and goes 1.8 miles to the lake.

To access Juanita Lake, from Highway 97 a couple of miles beyond Tennant Road, a paved road goes north 7 miles to the lake. It is clearly marked by a sign.

Although fishing is similar at Orr and Juanita, because of the relative difficulty of access, Orr gets much less pressure. The key for both lakes is weed growth. They are covered with weeds and lily pads, and the trout lurk in open areas, waiting for the many

insects that inhabit such growth.

Fred Gordon, a guide in Dunsmuir and one of the best fly-line anglers I've ever fished with, says Orr is one of his favorite stillwater spots.

"You can fish it early in the year, about the end of March, if the weather is good," he says. "The only problem is that it is full of weeds and lily pads, and you need to know where holes in the lily pads are. It's tough early in the season because the lily pads haven't grown up, but about the first of May, you can see them.

"The fish lie off the weed beds. Take a damsel imitation or a nymph such as a Pheasant Tail and hang it under an indicator. If you can see fish working, go down only about a foot and a half, but if there is no surface action, let your fly drop about five feet into the water."

Another possibility, Gordon says, is a bloodworm imitation that he ties in black, rather than red. He also says he's never found particularly good fishing early in the day – the action begins about 11 a.m. There are both rainbows and browns in Orr. The rainbows are stocked, but bigger holdover fish are common.

He also urges catch-and-release anglers to be extremely gentle with fish. There seems to be a high mortality rate, and anything that can be done to make it easy on released fish will help their survival.

Fishing Juanita requires the same setup, and both lakes can be fished either from a small pram or boat or with a float tube or pontoon boat. Fishing from shore isn't productive because of the weed growth.

THE BEST OF THE REST

Several other lakes in the area are worth mentioning, not because they are excellent wild-trout fisheries, but because they offer beautiful scenery along with fun fishing for stockers, mostly rainbows.

Castle Lake: It seems as if every angler you talk to in this area mentions Castle Lake. The refrain goes, "The fishin' is only so-so, but you have to see the scenery!" In fact, the fishing is pretty much for stocked rainbows, but the scenery is worth the 10-mile trip from I-5. It is a nice way to spend a day with the family. The kids can play in the water while you float tube around the lake and catch ten-inch or twelve-inch rainbows with worn-down fins. One of the reasons for Castle's beauty is that it is a glacial cirque lake, which means that it was formed in the depression left by a melting glacier.

It covers 1,900 surface acres and sits at 5,600 feet. It also is deep – 160 feet. For the record, the road generally is kept open in the winter, and ice fishing for trout is popular. To get to Castle Lake, take the West Lake Street exit from I-5 at the town of Weed, go south on W. A. Barr Road past Lake Siskiyou, then follow Castle Lake Road up the mountainside to the lake. Lake Siskiyou is a heavily stocked recreation area just off Interstate 5 where swimming, boating, and playing in the water are just as popular as fishing. There are lots of better places for fly fishers to go.

Gumboot Lake: This little mountain lake (seven surface acres) is becoming more and more popular with the locals, who try to keep it a secret. It is stocked, but the DFG is using larger rainbows, and there are a few wild rainbows. No motors are permitted, and although float tubing is ideal, it also can be fished from the bank. As with most of the lakes in this area, the scenery is just great.

September and October, when many trout anglers have packed it in for the year, can be a good time to fish. The bigger rainbows will cruise along the lily pads, and a fly fisher can walk the banks and spot fish. Otherwise, there are respectable caddis and mayfly hatches during the summer. For nymphs, beadheads in size 12 or 14 work well, drifted under an indicator or retrieved with a slow strip. Since Gumboot is only about thirteen feet deep, you don't need to get your flies that far down.

To get to Gumboot Lake, take the West Lake Street exit from I-5, go south on W. A. Barr Road past Lake Siskiyou, then turn right past the lake and follow the signs to Gumboot. It is about a 20-mile drive along the South Fork of the Sacramento River. There are several other mountain lakes nearby, but Gumboot is the best for fly fishing.

Bullseye Lake: This little fishery gets overlooked because it is so close to the much larger and more popular Medicine Lake. For the fly-line angler, Bullseye is a more rewarding stillwater than Medicine, which is home to thousands of small brookies dumped in by the Department of Fish and Game. The DFG also stocks both rainbows and brook trout in Bullseye, but since it is so much smaller, they are more concentrated. It is a shallow, five-acre lake that can be fished from shore, if need be. It also is high enough so that the road generally is not open until May because of snow. To get to Bullseye, take the McCloud exit off Interstate 5 just south of Mt. Shasta City, follow Highway 89 28 miles through the town of McCloud to Bartle, then go north 30 miles on Powder Hill Road (also marked as Forest Service Road 49) to the turnoff to the east to Bullseye Lake.

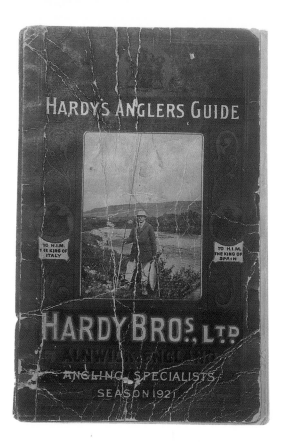

Resources

Fly shops in this area include:

■ **The Fly Shop**, 4140 Churn Creek Road, Redding, CA 96002, telephone (530) 222-3555, web site: www.theflyshop.com, e-mail: info@ theflyshop.com.

■ **Dunsmuir Flyfishing Company**, 5839 Dunsmuir Avenue, Dunsmuir, CA 96025, telephone (530) 235-0705.

■ **The Ted Fay Fly Shop**, 4310 Dunsmuir Avenue, Dunsmuir, CA 96025, telephone (530) 235-2969.

■ **Vaughn's Sporting Goods and Fly Shop**, 37307 Main Street, Burney, CA 96013, telephone (530) 335-2381.

■ **Trout Country**, near Burney on Highway 299, 38247 Main 299 East, Johnson Park, CA 96013, telephone (530) 335-5304.

The **Shasta Cascade Wonderland Association** offers details of lodging, camping, and just about anything else you might want to know about the area. It can be reached at 1699 Highway 273, Anderson, CA 96007, which, if you are driving to the area, is located near the Anderson factory outlet shopping center just off Interstate 5. Telephone (530) 365-7500, fax (530) 365-1258. Its web site is www.shastacascade .org, and e-mail is scwa@shastacascade.org.

Chapter 9

Big Lake, Eastman Lake, and Baum Lake

Baum Lake gets its share of fly-line anglers, but odds are, you've never even heard of Big Lake and Eastman Lake. Yet they are in the state's special-regulations program and hold multi-pound trout often caught by sight-fishing in gin-clear water.

The secret to these unknown fishing bonanzas? They are part of the fantastic Fall River system, a spring-fed cornucopia of slow-flowing, trout-jammed waterways in eastern Shasta County. Michael Dean, the Department of Fish and Game wild-trout biologist for the area, describes them as "the two least-known lakes in the Catch-and-Release Program."

As always seems to be the case, there also is bad news – at least for anglers who seek easy access. They are fishable only by boat, and access is limited. As a result, they are fished mostly by locals, while visiting anglers tend to flock to the better-known Fall River.

Baum Lake also is part of this ecosystem, which includes the Pit River and Hat Creek. This interconnected chain of waterways offers some of the best trout fishing in the Golden State.

Eastman Lake really is only a wide spot in the Little Tule River, but it offers prime fishing for big trout.

BIG LAKE
AND EASTMAN LAKE

Does your heart pound and do your hands tremble when you see cruising pods of big trout? Are you prone to hyperventilation or heart attacks? Then please don't come to these lakes, because the adrenaline level can be unbearable.

These are the kind of lakes I normally wouldn't ever tell anybody about, except that there are enough problems fishing them and catching the lunkers that live there that I feel secure they won't get pounded by droves of anglers.

The big drawback for most fly fishers is the access problem. There are two ways to get onto the lakes, which are about 6 miles apart, but connected by the Tule River. The first access, onto Eastman, is from Lava Creek Lodge, a resort that sits on this small lake. If you stay there, access is free. Otherwise, they

charge a launching fee. You also can rent a boat by the day or half-day, but both fees are fairly expensive, compared with what is charged at some of the big lakes where there are competing marinas.

Here's how to get to Lava Creek Lodge. As you enter the town of Fall River Mills on Highway 299, which goes east from Redding, turn north on Glenburn Road and go 6 miles to McArthur Road. Turn right on McArthur, then left on Island Road, and follow it almost three miles to the lodge. If you are coming from the east on 299, you can pick up McArthur Road in the town of McArthur, then turn north when you hit Island Road.

The second access is by way of a free boat ramp on Big Lake that can be reached from McArthur. To get to the Big Lake access, turn north from Main Street (Highway 299) where a sign says "Big Lake 4 Miles." Go

straight at a stop sign, past the rear of the fairgrounds, where the road turns to dirt (Rat Ranch Road is the official name), and proceed about a mile to the access. This also is the way to get to Ahjumawi Lava Springs State Park, which borders the northern side of the lake, and which can be reached only by boat.

As you'll see on some maps, Tule Lake lies between Eastman and Big Lakes. But for all practical purposes, it is considered part of Big Lake, and DFG regulations for this entire system are for a two-fish limit, but otherwise without special restrictions. In other words, barbed hooks and bait can be used.

By the way, you may have trouble finding these restrictions in the DFG's Sport Fishing Regulations booklet, and so did I. They are at the beginning of the "Trout, Salmon, and Special Regulations" section, rather than under the alphabetic listings of waters with special regulations.

Eastman "Lake" really is a wide spot in the Little Tule River and is surrounded by private houses and private land, with no access other than Lava Creek Lodge. There is a no-wake speed limit because it is so small. At the upper end of this quarter-mile-long lake, Lava Creek flows in over a barrier, creating a waterfall and tailout that draw a congregation of big trout. DFG biologists have snorkeled this area to check the fish population and found numerous trout in the twenty-five-inch range, along with dozens and dozens of smaller fish.

Obviously, it is the favorite spot to fish on Eastman, and just about every angler on the water holds there to drift flies or work lures through the tailout.

Frank Bertaina, co-owner of Lava Creek Lodge and a lifelong fly fisherman, points out that there are plenty of other areas to find big fish. The best bet, he says, is along the banks, where there are rock piles and where the fish gather in the shallower water to feed on sculpins. A Matuka or other streamer is the most effective way to get a strike from these lunkers.

"If I had to catch a fish over eight pounds, it would be by fishing in Eastman Lake," Bertaina says. "Ninety percent of the fish that are going to be caught here are caught on a streamer. There are lots of wild rainbows of five pounds caught every year."

While there aren't that many hatches, Bertaina says that there are some damsels, *Callibaetis*, and even caddis that will draw fish to the surface on occasion. However, unlike the Fall River itself, there is no major hatch of *Hexagenia limbata*, the huge yellow mayfly that pulls in big, hungry fish and can offer excellent dry-fly angling during midsummer evenings.

To get to Big Lake by boat, follow the Little Tule River from Eastman Lake, then bear left where the river forks – the right fork goes to Fall River.

Big Lake is much more lakelike than Eastman and is spread over hundreds of acres. But this is definitely not a stillwater where you can just pick a likely spot and start fishing. Although trout will sometimes scatter throughout the lake, they tend to concentrate at the northern edge, where a half-dozen or so huge springs pour in cold, clear, oxygenated water. The springs are located in inlets or bays, and an angler must creep into position to fish there.

The springs themselves look something like a bomb crater or a big bowl, with water coming up from the bottom. The flow is obvi-

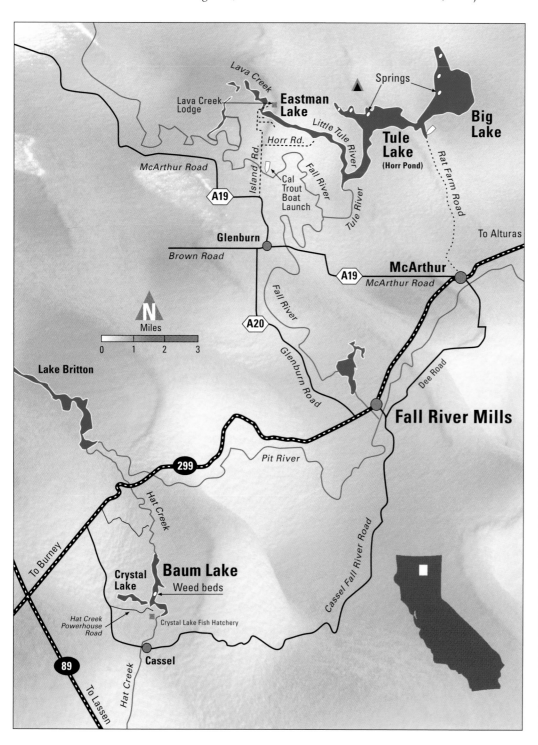

Frank Bertaina casts to one of the spring areas on Big Lake, where huge rainbows hang out in pods.

ous from the movement of under-water vegetation.

I can't emphasize enough: Don't go charging in with a motor running, or all you'll see are big trout squirting to safety. Use an electric trolling motor for the last several hundred feet. Fish your way into the area, working the edges and gradually getting deeper into the spring-water bays and inlets. Another way to do it is to carry along a float tube or pontoon boat and use it to fish the springs.

The fish often hold above or near the numerous rock piles that dot the bottom. The water is so clear that you can see the rocks from a distance – they look brown against the light-colored sand that makes up most of the lake bottom. Get close enough and you can see the fish, too. Unfortunately, they also can see you.

Long, light casts are necessary. The fish aren't really leader-shy (10 feet of 5X fluorocarbon is what Bertaina uses), but they are line-shy, so if you line them, say bye-bye and go to another spot. It is better to use a clear or camouflage-colored slow-sinking intermediate line, rather than one of those fluorescent floating lines that are so popular.

This is sight fishing for big trout at its best. Your heart will start pounding and your hands will tremble when you spot a pod of twenty-inchers cruising within casting distance. Just do everything perfectly (Yeah, right!) and you'll soon be hooked up to an enraged monster.

As at Eastman, streamers are the best way to catch fish here, although sometimes a nymph or emerging caddis imitation works well.

"If I had to catch a fish over eight pounds, it would be by fishing in Eastman Lake," says Frank Bertaina, co-owner of Lava Creek Lodge. "Ninety percent of the fish that are going to be caught here are caught on a streamer. There are lots of wild rainbows of five pounds caught every year."

Cinnamon
and olive leeches are
the most effective flies, along
with olive Matukas, all about size 6.
The best fishing is in the spring and
fall, although Bertaina says that
August also can be excellent, even if
there is a heavy algae bloom on the
lake that makes the water ugly.

BAUM LAKE

Baum Lake, like so many good stillwater fisheries, has about the same character as a spring creek – clear, cold, slow-flowing water and plenty of weed growth to pump out the insects on which trout feed. There is a primitive boat ramp, but no motors are allowed. It also can be fished by float tube or from the bank.

Baum, which covers about ninety surface acres, is next to the Crystal Springs Fish Hatchery. To get there, turn south off Highway 299 onto Cassel Road about 2 miles east of the Highway 299/89 junction, follow it for 2 miles, then go left on Hat Creek Powerhouse Road, which leads to the lake.

There are no special regulations on Baum, and it is heavily stocked with rainbows and browns by the DFG. But before you turn your nose up and mutter something about "wild trout," be aware that they grow fast and there are plenty of big holdovers to break the light tippets you'll need to use.

Baum is fed by water that comes from nearby Crystal Lake (more about fishing there later) and from the Hat #1 Powerhouse. After passing through the lake, the water goes to the Hat #2 Powerhouse and thence to the catch-and-release section of Hat Creek. Because the inflow and outflow is steady, a definite current flows all the way through the lake, giving it its spring-creek quality.

For anglers who want to fish from the shore, access is available near the parking lot, or they can walk along the trail that begins at the parking lot and follows a good portion of the western side of the lake. A float tube or pram is a better

Richard Burns picks a pattern to use on Baum Lake, which hosts a multitude of very selective fish.

Baum Lake can be fished from the shore, but a float tube or pram is better even though you'll have to fight the current.

way to go, allowing you to cover more water, particularly the productive weed bed area at about the midpoint of the lake. But remember that the flowing water that carries you oh-so-gently toward the dam will be against you on the trip back, so be prepared for some hard kicking or rowing.

Because of the prolific weed growth, insects abound. That's great for the fish, tough for the angler. Midges are a big item on the trout menu, and they range in size from about an 18 to a 24. Choose any dark midge pattern you like and you should do OK. However, you do need to present midges in the film or just under it with a light tippet, 6X or 7X, if you can deal with it, and a 12-foot leader.

Otherwise, there are numerous mayflies and caddisflies of different sizes and colors, but for the most part, they are small, so keep your imitations of both nymphs and

dries in the 16-to-18 size range. The standard patterns – PTs, Zug Bugs, Hare's Ears, for nymphs, and PMDs, plus the Adams and Elk Hair Caddis for dries – work fine. Don't forget black or olive Woolly Buggers or leeches for underwater work, either.

Baum is open to fishing year-round, and in the winter it can be at its best, particularly for anglers who enjoy fishing small midges for large trout. Otherwise, the spring and fall are good, with the summer, as usual, being the down season because of the heat.

A word about adjoining Crystal Lake: It also is heavily stocked, and since it doesn't have Baum's spring-creek current and weed growth, it is much easier to fish. It can be a good place for novice fly-line anglers to try their budding skills, but they'll have to share the water with the Power Bait crowd. As at Baum, no boats with motors are allowed.

Resources

The closest full-service fly shops are **Vaughn's Sporting Goods and Fly Shop**, 37307 Main Street, Burney, CA 96013, telephone (530) 335-2381, and **Trout Country**, near Burney on Highway 299, 38247 Main 299 East, Johnson Park, CA 96013, telephone (530) 335-5304 . **The Fly Shop** in Redding also keeps tabs on most waters in this area. It is at 4140 Churn Creek Road, Redding, CA 96002, telephone (530) 222-3555, web site: www.theflyshop.com, e-mail: info@theflyshop.com.

Lava Creek Lodge also has flies and some other gear. The telephone is (530) 336-6288, fax is (530) 336-1087, and its web site is www.lavacreeklodge.com. The address is Glenburn Star Route, Fall River Mills, CA 96028.

The **Fall River Mills Chamber of Commerce** can help with information on camping, lodging, and so on. Their phone is (530) 336-5840, and their address is 43107 Highway 299 East. If you think you're in the wrong place, you're not – they really are in the Valley Market. The mailing address is P.O. Box 475, Fall River Mills, CA 96028.

Chapter 10

Eagle Lake

Jay Fair is synonymous with Eagle Lake – he's been fishing and guiding on its waters for decades.

Eagle Lake, in Lassen County in northeastern California, is California's best big-trout stillwater fishery. That said, fishing it isn't easy. You have to be in the right place at the right time of year, know how to present your fly, and often be willing to brave elements that make you wish you were at home in front of a warm fire.

Eagle Lake is a special place. Not only is it the second-largest natural lake in the state (Tahoe doesn't count because half of it is in Nevada, so Clear Lake is first), but it is home to a special strain of native rainbow trout, *Oncorhynchus mykiss aquilarum*. Commonly known as Eagle Lake trout, they are the only trout able to survive in the lake's highly alkaline waters and are such a successful game fish that they now are planted in numerous streams and lakes across the state, including such stillwaters

"I catch 70 percent of my fish wading from shore," says Jay Fair. "It is amazing how shallow the water will be where these big fish can be found. They'll be in two feet of water. Sometimes you can see one tailing and have to fish them on your knees."

as Lake Davis and Lake Almanor.

Several streams flow into Eagle Lake, most notably Pine Creek, at the northwestern side of the lake, near Spalding (sometimes spelled Spaulding). But there is no outflow – only evaporation lowers the water level. This is why the water is much more alkaline than in other lakes that have a steady inflow-outflow of fresh water.

Greed almost wiped out this wonderful species of trout and turned Eagle Lake into a glorified mud puddle. California's water politics being what it is, the feeling was that all that fine water was going to waste just sitting in the lake. So in 1929, a business group drilled a tunnel through the mountain at Miners Point on the eastern side to provide irrigation to farmers in the Honey Lake area southeast of Susanville. The water level dropped thirty-three feet,

To Alturas

Cleghorn Creek

Stone Road

Stones
Landing

Pine Creek

Half Moon Bay

Rocky Point

Buck Bay

Buck Point

Troxel Point

139

Spalding

Airstrip

Eagle Lake

Little Troxel Point

To Susanville

Pelican Point

Eagle Lake Road

A1

Wildcat
Point

Eagle
Lake
Marina

Gallatin Beach

Eagle's
Nest

Tunnel

Miners Point

Gallatin Road

Papoose Creek

Merrill Creek

N

Miles

0   1   2   3

To Susanville

The best fishing on Eagle Lake is in the fall and early winter when the weather is cold, wet and miserable.

decreasing the surface area from 29,000 to 16,000 acres, and the alkalinity level went sharply up.

The number of fish decreased rapidly. Luckily for the species, the water company went bankrupt, and the outflow of water was stopped. Even so, by 1949, there were only a handful of fish left. The species was saved when the California Department of Fish and Game trapped a few of them as they sought to spawn in Pine Creek and spawned them in a hatchery. When the fish grew to maturity, the DFG replanted nearly two hundred of them into the lake. From that tenuous beginning, Eagle Lake has been restocked with its native fish and today is a blue-ribbon stillwa-

ter destination for anglers.

DFG biologists annually take around 3,000,000 eggs from close to 1,000 prime females. Nearly 200,000 of the hatchery-raised rainbows in the twelve-inch class are later put back into the lake to replace those that have been caught and those that have died from natural causes.

The alkalinity that makes it tough for non-native species to survive in Eagle Lake also means that the water is loaded with minerals, which support a phenomenal number of insects and other aquatic life. The result is that in their native waters, the Eagle Lake rainbows grow fast and huge.

In 1998, Eagle Lake became part of the

"Although it has its ups and downs — good one year and perhaps slacking off the next year — I don't know where you can catch big trout on flies anyplace like it."

state's Heritage Trout Program, which was started by the Department of Fish and Game to protect and revive populations of native trout. For half a century, the Eagle Lake trout had survived only through the auspices of the DFG because there was no place to spawn. Until the 1920s, they could use Pine Creek for spawning water. Although it dries up in the lower reaches every year, there is enough flowing water in the upper creek for the fry to survive until the next season again fills the creek.

First the tunnel and later drought made access to the creek impossible, so the lake's trout could not spawn. In the 1940s, brook trout were planted in Pine Creek and pretty much took over. By the time the lake level had returned to the point where the Eagle Lake strain could go up the creek to spawn, the brookies were so established that the Eagle Lake fry, when hatched, could not compete well enough to survive. This is changing, and Eagle Lake may again

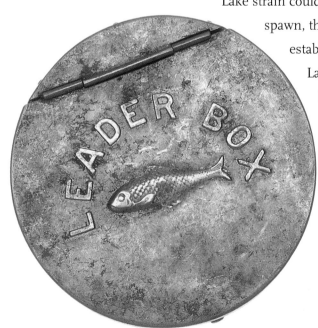

have a population of native wild trout. Private and public organizations teamed up to do major restoration work on the 20-mile lower stretch of Pine Creek that leads to about 8 miles of spawning water. Now the DFG is eradicating the brookie population so the Eagle Lake fry can survive in the creek.

Eagle Lake is at 5,100 feet above sea level, covers about 29,000 surface acres when full, and has more than 100 miles of shoreline, much of it heavily timbered. It runs vaguely north-south and is divided into three sections. The southern section is the largest and deepest, averaging about 60 feet. There's a section at the Eagle's Nest on the eastern shore that at about 100 feet is the deepest part of the lake. This also is the area where the trout tend to go in the summer when the water warms up, and it is where they hold during cold winter freezes.

The middle and northern sections are shallower and hence more productive for fly fishers because of the heavy weed growth. The middle section is about 20 feet deep, while the northern part is a bit shallower. They are separated by a narrows at Buck's Point.

"The trout probably average four pounds and run from three up to seven pounds. If there is plenty of water in the lake, they'll get even bigger."

Jay Fair with an average-sized Eagle Lake rainbow. Yup ... average sized.

HOW TO FISH EAGLE LAKE

You can't talk about Eagle Lake fly fishing without talking about Jay Fair. He has been fishing Eagle Lake for more than a quarter of a century, has been a fly fisher for sixty-five years, and still is going strong and still guiding as he nears eighty.

To top it off, he is truly a nice man, generous, open with advice, and always willing to help. He is a self-described fishaholic and doesn't consider a day complete unless he has put his line in the water. When

Jay Fair talks about how to fish Eagle Lake (or any other place, for that matter), it pays to listen.

"Eagle Lake is one of the top-notch lakes in the whole Western Hemisphere, so far as growing big trout," he says. "They are an extremely hard-fighting trout. They fight so hard they tend to kill themselves.

"Although it has its ups and downs – good one year and perhaps slacking off the next year – I don't know where you can catch big trout

on flies anyplace like it. The trout probably average four pounds and run from three up to seven pounds. If there is plenty of water in the lake, they'll get even bigger."

Fair became famous as a guide by trolling flies from a boat, an extremely effective method of catching fish that could be done by inexperienced anglers. However, his preferred method of fly fishing is wading, which is how he guides with capable fly-line anglers.

What he does is get on the water

A Jay Fair Special in his favorite color, burnt orange. He tied it for Eagle Lake, but it's effective on many stillwaters.

at first light and fish the weed beds in the central and northern sections of the lake. His advantage is his intimate knowledge of the lake.

"I catch 70 percent of my fish wading from shore," he says. "It is amazing how shallow the water will be where these big fish can be found. They'll be in two feet of water. Sometimes you can see one tailing and have to fish them on your knees."

Fair says that about 10 percent of Eagle Lake holds 90 percent of its fish. He singles out the best section as the northern end of the lake, which is paralleled for several miles by Highway 139 on the east and Eagle Lake Road on the west. There is weed growth throughout this entire area, perfect terrain for the wading fly fisher. It is easily accessed by parking alongside the road and walking to the water, which is close enough to carry a float tube if you want to go that route.

Other good areas are the shoreline just south of the airport at Spalding, Buck Point, Rocky Point at the northwestern end of the lake, and Wildcat Point in the southwestern corner.

Station yourself so you can cast along the edge of the weeds or into the open areas found in the weed beds. Eagle Lake is clear, so spotting fish is not difficult. The big fish, four pounds and up, are loners, and try to keep other fish out of their turf. Smaller fish, if you can call a three-pound trout small, will gather in pods of four or five fish.

The food base in Eagle Lake is pretty much the same as in other big California lakes – damselfly and dragonfly larvae, scuds, minnows, mayflies, and caddisflies. Snails also are an important food for trout, and there are times when they gorge on them.

Terry Edelmann, a Redding fly tier, says that occasionally he has run across what seems like millions of snails attached to the surface film from below, with big trout enjoying a gourmet dinner of escargot without the garlic, butter, and parsley. An effective way to fish during this period is to cast a snail or leech pattern into the area where the snails are holding – "the fish will hit it on the surface or when it begins to sink."

For the most part, this is nymph fishing – you don't get much chance to use dries. Fair swears by flies tied with a grizzly hackle dyed burnt orange, rust, or olive. Although many of his Woolly Bugger-style flies are tied on traditional 3X-long hooks, he also ties some flies on a short, size 10 scud hook because he believes the shorter hook is effective in keeping the tail from wrapping around the hook, which destroys the effectiveness of the fly. The sparse marabou tail should be at least as long as the hook on all the flies.

His snail imitation is tied on a scud hook with a peacock-colored crystal chenille that Fair calls "shuck" and a bushy tail that is cut off short, only about a quarter of an inch long. He lets it sink into the deeper holes, then pulls it back up a short distance and lets it sink again.

Fair says that when anglers miss strikes, they believe the trout has made a short strike – hitting just the tail and not taking the hook. Years of observation, he says, have proved to him that short strikes really don't happen. Trout inhale the whole fly, but spit it out so quickly that when the angler strikes, he or she believes the fish hasn't actually taken the fly.

As to general fishing technique, he says, "I get the fly to the bottom and let it wiggle around very slow. I think that presentation means more than the color of a fly. I use a real slow overhand retrieve. I just put the rod tip on the water and twitch it. You have to keep a tight line – the biggest problem is that unless an angler fishes a lot, it is awfully hard to detect when the fish take the fly. They'll suck it in with one breath and out with the next."

Fair says that for fishing water up to about six feet deep, he puts sixteen wraps of .015-inch lead on the fly and uses a floating line. Deeper than that, he uses a slow-sinking intermediate line. "Just count it down and get it near the bottom and twitch it along."

Even before Eagle Lake became part of the state's Heritage Trout Program, the limit for taking trout in Eagle had been reduced from five fish to two, where it remains today. All methods of fishing, including the use of bait, are legal. The season is open from the Saturday before Memorial Day through December 31, but there is only a brief window of opportunity early in the season. Usually by July, the water has warmed up enough so that most of the fish have headed for the deeper southern portion of the lake and are out of reach of the fly-line angler.

That means that the best fishing opportunities occur as cold weather sets in. During October, the water temperature drops below 60 degrees, and the fish return to the central and northern sections of the lake. From then until the season closes on December 31, the fish are there – the question is whether an angler is willing to brave the often numbingly cold elements to try to catch them.

In November and December during a cold year, ice on the shallower portions of the lake will pretty much put an end to fishing, although boats still can be launched at the southern ramps if you are willing to take a chance on sliding into the water on ice-slick concrete.

And be warned: Eagle Lake is a big lake, and winds can quickly whip up that make it extremely dangerous at any time of year. A number of anglers have lost their lives on the lake when caught in bad weather.

The best fishing occurs for about an hour in the morning, just as it gets light. Fair says there is another hour-long burst of feeding activity along about 11:30 a.m. If the lake is dead calm, with sun glaring on the water, the fish may wait until enough breeze comes up to riffle the top of the water and give them a better sense of protection.

As for gear, use a heavy enough rod to cast in a wind and to handle big fish – a 6-weight is about right. Leaders should be 12 feet and heavy, 3X or 2X. Fair notes that while the fish aren't leader-shy, they are line-shy, and colorful, fluorescent lines can scare them. He uses clear or camouflage lines.

Fair also has one other important suggestion: Treat the fish you catch very gently, because they have a high mortality rate. He urges catch-and-release anglers not to take big fish out of the water, even for photographs. He believes a very high percentage of fish taken from the water for only a few seconds die, even if they are able to swim away from the angler.

"When you fish as long as I have, you develop a reverence for fish. I hate to see a trout that's fought his life out for you die."

HOW TO GET TO EAGLE LAKE

The closest town is Susanville, 14 miles south of Eagle Lake. Susanville is 134 miles east of Redding via Highway 44 off Interstate 5. From the east, Susanville is 80 miles north of Reno on Highway 395.

To get to Eagle Lake from Susanville, take Highway 139 from the center of town about 30 miles to the north shore. To get to the south shore, take Highway A1 (Eagle Lake Road) north from Highway 36, 2 miles west of Susanville. It is about 14 miles to the lake.

From either Highway 139 or Highway A1, the western shore of the lake is accessed by Eagle Lake Road / Highway A1. The town of Spalding is about halfway along the west shore and is accessible along a 2-mile road. There is a boat ramp and an airport at Spalding. There also are boat ramps at Eagle Lake Marina and Gallatin Beach in the south and at Stone's Landing in the north. All are free.

Resources

Fishing tackle and information: There aren't any sporting-goods or fly shops in the Eagle Lake area, but Jay Fair sells some essential equipment and his own flies from his home in Spalding. His home is at 687-900 Linden Way, just off The Strand. His telephone is (530) 825-3401.

For information on fishing conditions, the Eagle Lake RV Park generally will answer questions. It can be reached at (530) 825-3133.

Campgrounds: There are private and public campgrounds scattered around the lake. Information on the four U.S. Forest Service campgrounds at the southern end of the lake can be obtained from the U.S. Forest Service's Eagle Lake Ranger District at 477-050 Eagle Lake Road, Susanville, CA 96130, telephone (530) 257-4188. However, reservations must be made through the National Recreation Reservation System at (877) 444-6777. Information also can be obtained on their web site, www.reserveUSA.com.

There is a small U.S. Bureau of Land Management campground at the northern end of the lake. The BLM office is at 2950 Riverside Drive, Susanville, CA 96130, telephone (530) 257-0456. This is a first-come, first-served campground.

Lake Almanor offers a few weeks of exciting fly fishing during its annual *Hexagenia* hatch. Apart from that ... well, it's a big, popular resort lake with speedboats, water-skiers, sailing, and all the other water sports.

There are lots of brawny trout in Almanor, a few of them wild, most of them planters or holdovers. At certain times and places, they can be caught by fly-line anglers. For the most part, however, trolling lures or dunking bait produces the lunkers, which usually hold deep during the warm months.

There are numerous alternatives for the fly fisher within an hour's driving distance or less. Butt Valley Reservoir, just 4 miles west of Lake Almanor, used to have, and should have again, good fishing. McCoy Flat Reservoir and its neighbor, Hog Flat Reservoir, can provide excellent fishing. For those who enjoy spectacular scenery, Crater Lake, Silver Lake, and Echo Lake offer brookies and rainbows, some of them in the sixteen-inch range. For anglers who don't mind doing a bit of easy hiking, the Caribou Wilderness has more than a dozen lakes with fish, several of them less than an hour's walk from the trailhead.

There is a plethora of fun fishing here, but let's be honest, most of these lakes are not blue-ribbon lunker-trout waters. Apart from the annual Hex hatch, those seeking twenty-inchers are better off going to nearby Eagle Lake and pitting their skills against its famed strain of native rainbow trout. (See the preceding chapter.)

For the purpose of orientation, I'll use the town of Chester at the northern end of Lake Almanor as a starting point. Because some of the lakes are closer to Susanville, I'll also give distances and directions from there.

Since Lake Almanor is the centerpiece of this chapter, let's deal with it first.

The striking yellow Hexagenia limbata *is the largest of the mayflies found in California.*

Lake Almanor's Hex hatch, which comes at dusk in late June and early July, is one of the most exciting stillwater fishing experiences in California.

LAKE ALMANOR

To be up-front about it, I'm just not a fan of big, popular recreational lakes, no matter how good the fishing. It upsets me to be quietly float tubing in a cove and suddenly have a boatload of vacationing teenagers come charging into the area. They have as much right to the cove as I do, but why put myself in this position when there are other, quieter places more suited to what I enjoy as a fishing experience?

On the flip side of the coin, sometimes the fishing is just so good it doesn't make any difference. And that's the case with the annual Hex hatch at Lake Almanor. It helps that the hatch takes place at dusk, when most of the boating traffic already is off the lake.

Almanor's Hex hatch is an angling experience not to be missed. *Hexagenia limbata* is the largest of the mayflies, living in the muddy or sandy bottom of slow-moving streams or lakes and then emerging to mate and lay eggs for a new generation. While there are Hex hatches on other California stillwaters, the one on Lake Almanor is perhaps the best known.

While temperature, weather, and other factors all influence the timing of the Almanor hatch, it generally begins around mid-June and lasts for several weeks, traditionally peaking around the Fourth of July. It draws all types of anglers, but it is perfect for fly fishers.

The hatch starts as the sun goes down, around 8:45, and lasts for only about forty-five wild minutes. The main spots for the hatches are in coves with mud bottoms, of which there are many in Lake Almanor. Favored areas are the west and east banks at the southern end of the lake, or even in the marshy area near the bridge that crosses the

Almanor's Hex hatch is an angling experience not to be missed. *Hexagenia limbata* is the largest of the mayflies, living in the muddy or sandy bottom of slow-moving streams or lakes and then emerging to mate and lay eggs for a new generation. While there are Hex hatches on other California stillwaters, the one on Lake Almanor is perhaps the best known.

You need to have some patience. With all the slurping and splashing of the big fish rising around you, the tendency is to start wildly throwing your fly to wherever the latest action is. Adrenaline flow notwithstanding, you need to put your fly on the water and do the strip routine. Remember, you can't catch fish with your fly in the air.

lake near the town of Chester at the northern end. The most popular spot is at the boat ramp at the southwestern end of the lake, which has a sandy beach that makes it easy for float tubers.

Hexagenia emerge from the mud and slowly make their way to the surface, where they pop out of their shucks and become winged mayflies. They sit on the surface for a few seconds, waiting for their wings to dry and stiffen, and then they attempt to fly. Most of the time, they don't make it into the air on their first attempt, skittering across the surface for six or eight inches. If they don't get into the air, they rest a bit and then try again.

Imitate this with your fly. Toss it out, let it sit a few seconds, and then strip it for a few inches. Wait a bit and repeat the process. If fish are rising nearby, or you can tell which direction a feeding fish is headed, cast to a likely spot. Otherwise, just put it out there and keep the action going. The *Hexagenia* imitations need to float high and not be pulled under when you strip. I soak mine in Scotchgard and then gunk them up with a paste floatant.

You need to have some patience. With all the slurping and splashing of the big fish rising around you, the tendency is to start wildly throwing your fly to wherever the latest action is. Adrenaline flow notwithstanding, you need to put your fly on the water and do the strip routine. Remember, you can't catch fish with your fly in the air.

Rainbows, browns and bass all smash both nymphs and dries during the Lake Almanor Hex hatch.

Hex Cripples are effective on Lake Almanor during the Hexagenia hatch.

Takes are not subtle, so use strong leaders, 4X or 3X at least, and a rod heavy enough to be able to deal with fish that occasionally may weigh in double digits.

Hex imitations offered by Chester's two sporting-goods stores generally are tied on size 6 or size 4 hooks. Del Heacock, at Dr. Del's Fly Shop in Chester, has his own version of the Hex that he ties with a Mylar-thread wing that offers an excellent silhouette to the fish and is easy to spot for the angler, an advantage in low light. He ties it a bit smaller, on a size 10 hook. "I think that's more realistic as to the size of the flies," he says.

For a couple of hours before the hatch itself, using big, yellow Hex nymph imitations can be effective.

Tied on size 6 or size 8 hooks, these yellow flies can either be trolled or be cast out and left to sink, then retrieved with a short, slow strip that mimics the up-and-down action of the real thing as it makes its way toward the surface. There are more accurate imitations that can be purchased or tied, but a yellow Woolly Bugger or Woolly Worm will work just fine.

Float tubes and pontoon boats are excellent for the hatch, but small boats or even canoes also work. Larger boats rigged so you can cast a fly line will do, but you'll need to get set in the area you want to fish and not charge in with the motor cranked up, or you'll put the fish down. If you need to move about, do it with an electric motor.

When the hatch is in full flow, it seems as if everything is feeding on *Hexagenia* – trout, largemouth and smallmouth bass, bats by the hundreds, even ducks and other water birds, including seagulls.

Remember to take a large flashlight (as opposed to the small lights used to tie on flies) so you can warn away any boat that approaches and then use it when you get out of the water. It will be completely dark by the time you leave the lake.

So what about the other fifty or so weeks of the year? The good news is that Lake Almanor is full of big fish. The bad news is that for a fly-line type to catch them is, for the most part, tough going. This is a big lake – 16 miles long, 6 miles wide, covering 28,000 surface acres. It sits

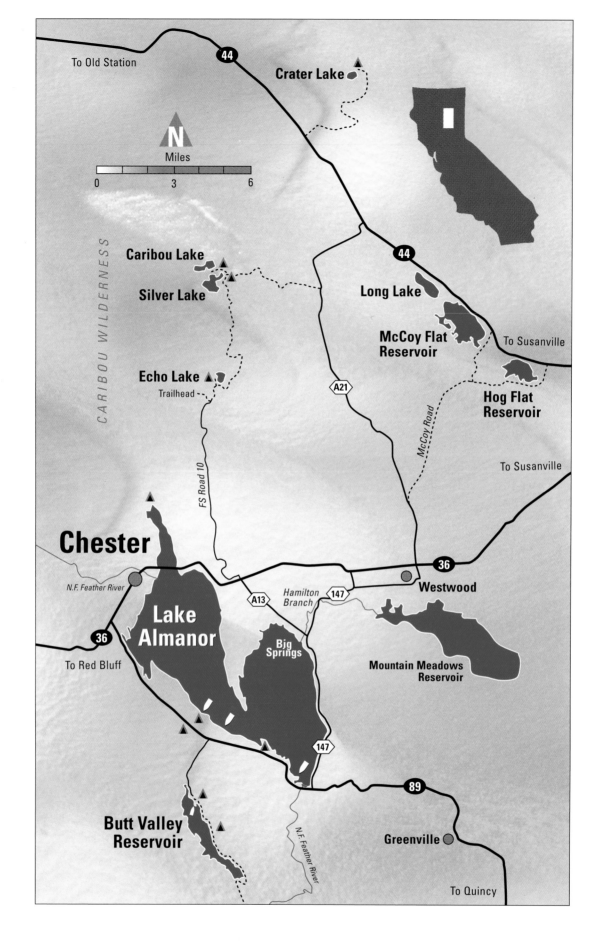

To Old Station

44

Crater Lake

N
Miles
0   3   6

CARIBOU WILDERNESS

Caribou Lake

Silver Lake

44

Long Lake

McCoy Flat
Reservoir

To Susanville

Echo Lake
Trailhead

A21

McCoy Road

Hog Flat
Reservoir

To Susanville

FS Road 10

Chester

N.F. Feather River

36

To Red Bluff

Lake
Almanor

Big
Springs

36

Westwood

A13   Hamilton   147
Branch

147

Mountain Meadows
Reservoir

147

89

Butt Valley
Reservoir

N.F. Feather River

Greenville

To Quincy

Butt Valley Reservoir, which has a mid-summer Hex hatch, is coming back as an excellent fishery after being drained for dam repairs.

at 4,510 feet altitude and is a perfect recreation spot, with hordes of vacationers flocking to the area. There are numerous summer homes and resorts around much of the lake, and there are no restrictions as to the use of boats or personal watercraft.

Bait-and-lure anglers do well at Almanor, mostly by trolling deep. For fly fishing, morning and evening are the best times, particularly in the spring or fall. The best areas are the northern arm near the Highway 36 causeway just outside Chester, in some of the coves on the southeastern or southwestern side of the lake, and where the Hamilton Branch of the Feather River flows in on the north shore.

The Hamilton Branch inlet is by far the most popular area for fishing, and rightly so, because fish stack up there. But that means it can

at times resemble a zoo, with so many boats that a fly-line angler in a float tube will feel like a pedestrian crossing Times Square at rush hour against the light.

Although there are occasional hatches, standard nymphs such as Pheasant Tails, Bird's Nests, and Zug Bugs, size 12 or 14, or olive or black Woolly Buggers are the preferred flies.

BUTT VALLEY RESERVOIR

Discussing Butt Valley Reservoir, which is only 4 miles west of Lake Almanor, presents a problem. For years, it offered as good fishing as Lake Almanor – it even had its own Hex hatch – but beginning in 1996, it was drawn down to almost nothing so the dam could be repaired. It took another couple of years to fill, and is slowly coming back, although still a ways from being as

good a fishery as before.

Fish were replanted in the lake. However, it has taken longer for the aquatic insect life to proliferate. Hexes began to show themselves in the summer of 2000, but the hatch needs another year or two to regain its former glory.

In other words, this is a place that, given a couple of more years, might provide good fishing, but at this point doesn't offer a lot to the fly fisher. An added benefit for fly-line anglers on Butt Reservoir is that it has a 5-mile-per-hour speed limit within 500 feet of the shore, which keeps most of the hotshot crowd off the reservoir.

The turnoff to Butt Valley Reservoir is west from Highway 89, which follows the west shore of Lake Almanor. It is a paved road that turns to gravel when it reaches the reservoir. The gravel road parallels the east shore of the lake and offers plenty of access. There is a launch ramp, and there are two campgrounds, Ponderosa Flat and Cool Springs.

The best fishing at Butt Valley Reservoir is in the summer, when the water is flowing in from Lake Almanor to produce power for PG&E. This powerhouse is at the northern end of the lake, and as water comes in, it brings minnows and other food. The result is logical: Big trout stack up to enjoy the feast.

Before the drawdown, there were some huge fish caught in this area, a few in the range of sixteen to seventeen pounds. Once things return to normal at Butt, those lunkers probably will be back in a few years, although they are tough to catch on a fly line.

McCOY FLAT RESERVOIR, LONG LAKE, AND HOG FLAT RESERVOIR

Fishing for big, holdover planters in this series of reservoirs alongside Highway 44 can be excellent. The first thing you need to know, however, is that the situation can change drastically from year to year, occasionally even from month to month.

The reservoirs are large and shallow, filling what used to be grassy meadows. They are shallow enough so that during a tough winter (the reservoirs are about 5,500 feet above sea level), they freeze solid, killing all the fish. That means no holdovers for the next fishing season, so all you'll be catching are the current year's planters.

A hot, dry summer can do the same thing – drawing the reservoirs down to skinny water hot enough to pretty much decimate the fish population. Again, that means there are no holdovers for the next year.

But whenever there are a couple of easy years when these reservoirs don't freeze or get low enough to become too hot, the trout grow like mad. There is a lot of food for them: mayflies, midges, caddisflies, scuds, damselflies, leeches – all those good things that go together to make up a yummy trout dinner.

The trout here can get trophy-

sized – ten-pounders have been caught and five-pounders come out regularly. There are rainbows, Eagle Lake strain rainbows, and browns in McCoy.

The trick to fishing the reservoirs is (surprise!) finding out where the fish are holding. In the spring and early summer, when fishing opens and the lakes are full and cold, the fish are scattered. They also are hungry, coming off a long winter. As the summer wears on, however,

the water becomes shallow, weed beds proliferate, and the trout seek the deeper holes and become more selective.

Anglers need to seek out these holes, which is one of the reasons those who fish here regularly usually do better. (When they find these spots, they aren't about to pass along the information.) The trout will stay in these deeper areas, usually marked by less vegetation, and forage for insects at the edge of nearby

McCoy Flat Reservoir is big and very shallow, but with the right conditions can offer large holdover rainbows.

weed growth. If you find one of these open areas in the weeds, fish it as you would any other weed bed – work along the edges with nymphs, scuds, or whatever insect seems to be plentiful at the moment.

Damselfly nymphs always are one of my favorites, but leech imitations, Woolly Buggers, mayflies, caddises, and midges in their varying stages also have to be on tap in your fly box.

McCoy Flat Reservoir is 18 miles from Susanville on Highway 44 (that's 97 miles from Redding, if you're coming that way), while Hog Flat Reservoir is a couple of miles nearer Susanville. To get to the reservoirs from Chester, follow Highway 36 east to A21 north, which takes you 18 miles to Highway 44. Go east on 44 to McCoy Flat or Hog Flat.

Access to McCoy Flat Reservoir is along a dirt road at the eastern end of the lake, where a sign says "Westwood 14." The road leads to the dam at the southeastern end of the lake. This is a favorite spot for bait anglers and also has a primitive boat-launch ramp.

If you continue along the dirt road, rather than turning off to the reservoir dam area, you'll wind around the southern end of the lake. There are a number of roads that lead to the bank and offer put-in areas for float tubers. A favored sec-

Echo Lake is easy to reach and is full of small brookies. Come prepared – the mosquitoes are vicious.

tion for some local fly fishers is the southwestern or western shore. It really is a matter of doing some exploring – probe the roads until you find a likely spot and then give it a try.

Hog Flat is a couple of miles east and has more limited access. Goumez Road on the east side of the lake is the way to the water. (On maps, this is listed as Conard Road.) It winds around the eastern and southern portion of the reservoir, with occasional dirt tracks going to the water.

The DFG does not stock Hog Flat, but apparently some fish have been put in there. This reservoir gets much less pressure than McCoy Flat and, according to some anglers, is a well-kept secret.

In any case, fish it the same as you would McCoy Flat – they have the same planted/holdover trout,

bugs, and weed growth. And if you get some big trout, don't tell anybody.

Long Lake, 5 miles west of McCoy Flat Reservoir on Highway 44, also holds fish. But it is the shallowest of the three reservoirs – few holes are more than six or eight feet deep – and as such is more susceptible to winter freezes and summer heat. Don't hesitate to give it a try. You could be pleasantly surprised, and chances are nobody will be fishing it.

CRATER LAKE

A half-dozen miles west of McCoy Flat on Highway 44 is the turnoff north to Crater Lake, a beautiful natural lake almost 7,000 feet high in the Lassen National Forest. It's a great place to camp, with water, toilets, tables, and scenic views. The only drawback is that the

7-mile gravel road from Highway 44 to the lake is like a washboard, so your vehicle and anything you are pulling will take a beating.

Like almost every lake in this area, it is pretty much hatchery-trout heaven. Both rainbows and brookies are planted, ranging in size from fingerlings to twelve-inchers. The fish, particularly the small brook trout, aren't hard to catch, and anglers can have a multifish, fun-filled day with a light rod.

Only non-motorized boats are allowed on the water. It isn't a big lake, only twenty-seven surface acres, and can be covered easily in a float tube.

SILVER LAKE

The turnoff to Silver Lake is 4 miles along Highway A21 going south from Highway 44 to Highway 36. It is an additional 6 miles on a gravel road to the lake, which is another of those pretty alpine lakes that dot the area. It has two campgrounds, Rocky Knoll and Silver Bowl, a picnic area, and is the most populated of the lakes around here, with a number of private shoreline homes.

Silver Lake is heavily planted with Eagle Lake rainbows, browns, and brookies, and because of this, many locals feel it offers the best fishing around. One thing is certain – you won't be alone on Silver Lake. Boating rules state that speedboaters and water-skiers are allowed to practice their sport only between the hours of 11 a.m. and 4 p.m. and that prior to 8 a.m., boating anglers can move at trolling speed only.

ECHO LAKE

Even though this lake is the most easily accessible (by paved road, no less!), it is my favorite for the area. There are no facilities – a toilet is the only amenity – and it has much less traffic than Silver or Crater. To top it off, I seem to catch more fish at Echo than anyplace else.

They are mostly brookies, ranging up to sixteen-inch holdovers, with a smattering of rainbows. Again, it is a pretty alpine lake, almost 7,000 feet high. It is a bit shallower than Silver or Crater Lakes, but still deep enough to keep some of the planters alive for the following year, and is about the same size as Crater Lake.

The reason few people visit here is that there are no signs leading the way. From Chester, go 5 miles east on Highway 36, then turn north on the road that goes to the Feather River Disposal site. This turnoff is easy to spot because it is directly across Highway 36 from the road to the east shore of Lake Almanor, which is clearly marked. The road ends in a T after a couple of hundred yards. Go left for 0.8 miles, then turn right on Forest Service Road 10.

This road is paved for the first 10 miles, but turns to gravel where the turnoff to the Caribou Wilderness is located. After about half a mile of gravel, the road forks – the right fork is a continuation of FS Road 10, which goes on to Silver Lake, if you want to go that way, while the left branch (actually it goes straight) continues another half a mile to Echo Lake. Be warned – this is mosquito country, so come prepared.

CARIBOU WILDERNESS AREA

This wilderness area is adjacent to Lassen Volcanic National Park, and as such has no amenities – it is a hike-in, pack-it-out area. For fly-line anglers who like to do a bit of walking, it is a fun place to spend a day without rigorous hiking.

The trailhead parking for the wilderness area is 2 miles from where the paved road that leads to Echo Lake ends. (See above.) There are a dozen lakes containing fish that are within hiking distance, several of them only a forty-five-minute walk away. None of the fish are big, though, as far as I know. Hidden Lakes, Long Lake, and Beauty Lake are the largest. If you can, pack along a float tube.

Another way into the Caribou Wilderness Area is from Silver Lake. Follow the road to Caribou Lake (yes, it has trout too), which is the jumping-off point for another batch of lakes.

There really are so many lakes in this area that it becomes impossible to mention all of them. However, the lakes that are stocked by airplane by the California Department of Fish and Game are Triangle, Evelyn, Posey, Hidden, Cypress, Gem, Eleanor, Rim, and Emerald.

Anybody who plans to do some serious hiking in the area needs to get a topographical map, which can be picked up from one of the area U.S. Forest Service stations. (See Resources, right.)

Resources

Fly shops in this area include:

■ **Dr. Del's Fly Shop**, 160 Main Street, Chester, CA 96820, telephone (530) 258-2980.

■ **Ayoob's Sports** has some fly-fishing gear available. It is located at 201 Main Street, Chester, telephone (530) 258-2611.

The **Plumas County Visitor's Bureau** offers details on camping and just about anything else you need to know about the area. It can be visited at 550 Crescent Street, Quincy, CA 95971 or telephoned at (800) 326-224, fax (530) 283-5465. Its web site is www.plumas.ca.us, and the e-mail is plumasco@psln.com.

The **Chester-Lake Almanor Chamber of Commerce** is at 529 Main Street, Chester, CA 96020. The telephone is (800) 350-4838 or (530) 258-2426, fax (530) 258-2760.

U.S. Forest Service stations in this area include **Lassen National Forest**, 55 South Sacramento Street, Susanville, CA 96130, telephone (530) 257-2151, and the **Almanor Ranger District**, 900 East Highway 36, Chester, CA 96020, telephone (530) 258-2141.

Chapter 12

Lake Davis and Frenchman Lake

Despite its infestation with northern pike, Lake Davis remains one of California's top trout stillwaters, a first-rate fishery that offers fly-line anglers a plentiful supply of fast-growing rainbows. Davis is one of those spots where the Department of Fish and Game dumps in thousands of hatchery fish. There are no special regulations, and some of the planters quickly end up in the frying pan. Those that remain gorge themselves on a variety of bugs and quickly grow to feisty twenty-inchers.

In theory, Davis can be fished year-round. In fact, it is snowed in and covered with ice during the winter, which means ice fishing is about the only attraction – and that's not exactly prime fly fishing. Beginning with ice-out and continuing until snow again clogs the road to the lake, it is a Mecca for fly-line types. Although best in the spring and fall, fishing can be good even during the summer months.

Frenchman Lake, a few miles to the east, also has had its problems with pike. Like Davis, it was poisoned with rotenone by the Department of Fish and Game to kill all the fish and then restocked. Its rehabilitation took several years, but it is back to normal.

Frenchman doesn't have the same high reputation among fly fishers as Davis. However, it is visited regularly by fly-line anglers from Nevada – it is only a half-hour drive from Reno – and they usually do quite well. So maybe Californians are missing a bet. It certainly is worth a try when Davis is slow.

Lake Davis can offer prime fishing in the late fall, as David Frazier demonstrates.

LAKE DAVIS

Northern pike are the nemesis of Lake Davis. These predatory fish were introduced illegally and began showing up in numbers in 1994. In 1997, the DFG, fearing the pike would escape downstream and spread to other waterways, proposed poisoning the entire lake to kill all the fish, then restocking it with trout. Since there are no spawning areas in Davis, and hence no wild trout, it was a feasible idea. But it touched off a firestorm, particularly in the nearby town of Portola, which draws some of its drinking water from Lake Davis.

Lawsuits, court actions, and general ill-will followed. It was resolved, not necessarily amicably, and the DFG used rotenone to poison the lake in October 1997. The poison did not dissipate as quickly as had been hoped, and the DFG was forced to keep Davis closed to fishing the following year, a public-relations disaster that touched off another round of lawsuits.

When it reopened in 1999, it quickly regained its status as a first-rate fishery. Then the pike showed up again. Nobody knows whether some misguided soul put them back in or if the poisoning for some reason failed to kill all the fish. Because of the recriminations over the original poisoning, the DFG discarded the idea of using rotenone again, although legally it remained an option. Instead, it has sought to keep the pike population under control by other means.

So far, it appears to have worked, but if pike ever get to the point where they are big enough to decimate the trout population, the DFG will have to rethink its course of action.

In the meantime, fishing Davis is a great stillwater experience. While anglers who work at matching the hatch and have lake-fishing expertise will do better, novice and intermediate fly fishers usually will do just fine, too. It is mostly a rainbow fishery, with Eagle Lake strain trout and a rainbow-kokanee hybrid.

Jay Fair, the doyen of fly-fishing guides in northeastern California, has a special place in his heart for Davis.

"Lake Davis is a real sweetheart, a jewel of a lake," he says. "The west side is tamarack trees, we call them lodgepoles, and the grass is absolutely gorgeous. There are hundreds of nesting geese, all sorts of wildlife. And there are big weed beds, all the types of water you'd want. It is one of those lakes where you feel good just being on the lake."

The usual brands of trout food are plentiful, and it has an exceptional population of snails on which the trout love to gorge. It can be an amusing surprise to take a large trout from your net and feel its belly stuffed with snail shells. And if you keep a trout for dinner, look at the stomach contents – you'll be amazed at how many snail shells it can hold.

Damselflies also are prime fare for Davis Lake trout, along with caddisflies, mayflies, and the rest of the smorgasbord that makes these fish grow so fast they look like footballs with small heads.

Although Woolly Buggers or leech patterns work as a snail imitation, Jay Fair ties his own artificial, the same one he uses at Eagle Lake.

"I use a scud hook with peacock 'shuck' and then put a fairly bushy tail on the fly and cut it off short, about a quarter-inch long. I let it fall into potholes, then raise it and let it drop again."

He notes that although damselfly patterns can be effective, "sometimes there will be lots of damsels, but trout will be feeding on Blood Midges.

"When fishing damsels, don't forget they change color. Start with medium olive tied on a short hook with a long tail – with a standard-length hook the tail will wrap

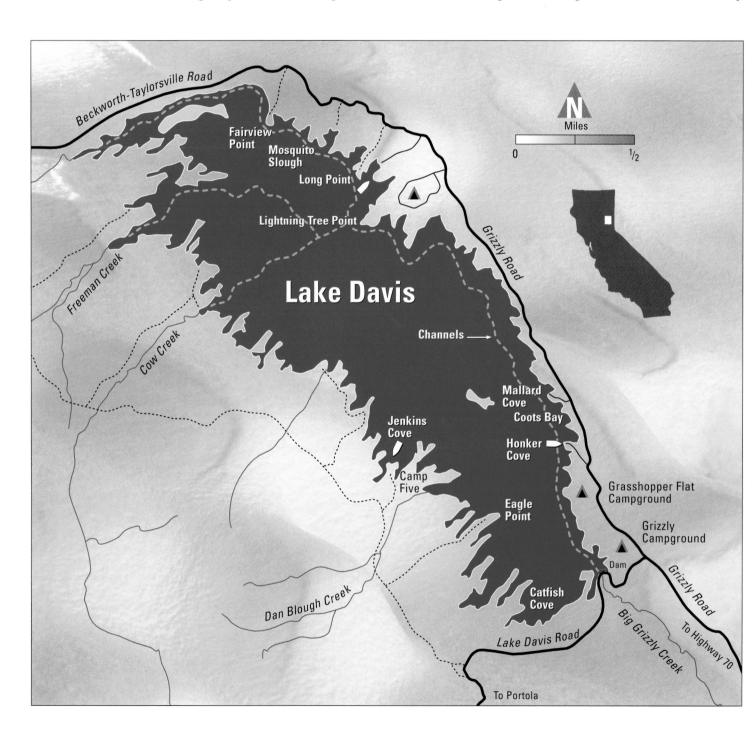

Alan Tegethoff admires a typical rainbow taken from Lake Davis, one of the favorite California stillwaters for fly-line anglers.

around the fly. If they are feeding on damsels and won't hit my fly, I'll go to sort of a tan damsel color. It helps a lot."

Ice-out is a prime time to fish Davis, as it is with many high-mountain lakes. The road to Davis, which sits at 5,775 feet, usually opens up sometime in April. Where anglers fish depends on what area they can access. Usually, the coves at the southwest end of the lake are the first to clear of snow, and casting from shore works just fine.

The trout tend to gather in the coves not only to feed, but in response to the urge to find an inlet and swim upstream to spawn. The fly of the day is a size 14 Brassie or some other midge imitation. Toss it out and let it sit, or make a slow, slow, slow retrieve.

If the road along the eastern shore is open, anglers can get to Mallard or Honker Coves, both of which have boat ramps. You also

can float tube, of course, but be sure to wear your long johns, because the water will be icy.

Damselflies come into their own in May and June with prolific hatches that draw the attention of cruising trout. These hatches don't begin early in the day, so there is no need to be there at dawn. Have a leisurely breakfast and then get on the lake by about 9 a.m. Damselfly nymphs in a size 12 or 14 are the ticket. As for color, early in the hatch, the nymphs tend to be fairly dark olive, then the bugs lighten to brown or gold as the day wears on.

Anglers who fish Davis regularly believe that just letting a damselfly nymph imitation sit a few inches below the film and giving it an occasional twitch is the best way to go. But if you troll or do a slow retrieve, you'll also be eligible for a multifish day. No light tippets, please, or you'll be breaking fish off regularly.

During this time, the coves along

the western shore of the lake are favorite spots for tubing. They are shallow and weedy, great areas for fish to cruise and look for edibles.

Damselfly imitations remain a good fly throughout the summer, along with caddisfly and mayfly patterns. There are numerous hatches, so use your eyes and offer them something approximating whatever is on the water. You'll find that Hare's Ears, Pheasant Tails, Zug Bugs, and Bird's Nests, size 12 to 16, usually will work well for nymphs, while an Adams and an Elk Hair Caddis, size 12 to 18, make good standbys for dries. Use the smaller versions later in the year. And always be willing to give leech patterns and Woolly Buggers a try. Cinnamon, olive, and black are the best colors, and anything from size 6 to size 10 may work. Both of these patterns offer a passable imitation of a snail to trout.

In September and into October,

when the weather is changing, the trout go into a feeding frenzy to stock up for winter, cruising the shallow water to eat anything they can find. It is one of the best times of year to fish Lake Davis, but that cold weather can bring early snow, so be prepared to be wet and cold. Bigger flies, particularly those Woolly Buggers and leeches, are the best bet then, even as big as a size 2 or 4.

Davis is 6 miles north of the town of Portola, which is on Highway 70 about 25 miles west of the intersection with Highway 395. It also can be reached via Grizzly Road, which intersects with Highway 70 about 3 miles east of Portola.

Davis is a good-sized lake, covering 4,026 surface acres. There are boat launch ramps at Honker Cove, Mallard Cove, and Lightning Tree on the east shore and at Old Camp Five on the west shore. The Grizzly Store and campground are at the southern end of the lake, and there are several Forest Service campgrounds scattered along the eastern shore.

A paved road follows the eastern shore, while a gravel road goes along the western shore and around the northern end of Lake Davis. A number of turnoffs lead to the various coves that dot the western shore. Any of these coves offers a good place for a float tuber to launch. There is no speed limit for boats on Davis, but water-skiing is not permitted.

FRENCHMAN LAKE

This is one of those high-desert lakes that don't get no respect, but in reality, it can supply some pretty good fishing. While Davis is surrounded by evergreens and shaded campgrounds, Frenchman sits in the middle of the sagebrush, with hardly a tree in sight.

What they do share is pike. Frenchman gained a bit of notoriety in 1987 when an angler caught a northern pike, a fish not supposed to be in California waters. Since it was poisoned with rotenone and restocked, it supposedly has remained clear of pike, unlike Davis.

Frenchman is at 5,599 feet above sea level and is smaller than Davis, with 1,580 surface acres. It has upper and lower sections, with a channel connecting them. The upper section, with shallow coves and summer weed beds, is the preferred area for fly fishers.

A gravel road goes all around the lake, and there are a number of side roads that offer fishing access. A three-lane boat ramp is at the southeastern end of the lake, and there are five campgrounds scattered around Frenchman. Those who camp in the area tend to be bait-and-lure anglers from Nevada. Boat launching can become difficult late in the summer, when the water level drops below the concrete ramp. There are no boating speed limits or restrictions.

Like Davis, this reservoir is heavily stocked with rainbows, including Eagle Lake trout, along with some browns and brookies (not to mention catfish and Kamloops trout). There is plenty of food for them to grow, but Frenchman is not quite as prolific as Davis.

Two of the better access points for fly-line anglers are on the northwestern shore, Snallygaster Point and Nightcrawler Bay. They are big, shallow areas with weed growth where the fish cruise to slurp up bugs. Use the same flies and techniques as you would at Davis.

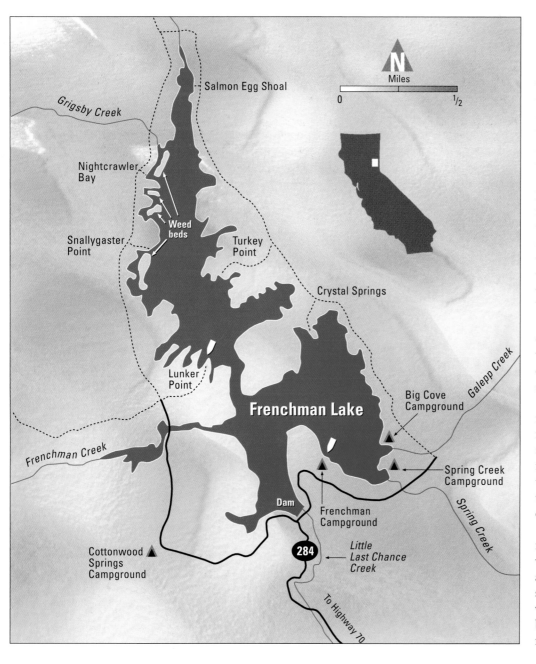

Frenchman Lake is popular with anglers from nearby Nevada and often is overlooked by California fly fishers. Steve Ottesen, from Reno, hits it regularly after work.

Although it is open year-round, ice, wind, and cold make it impossible to fish Frenchman in the winter. It is more open than Davis, and can quickly become dangerous in a high wind.

The turnoff to Frenchman from Highway 70 is at the little town of Chilcoot, which is about 5 miles west of Highway 395 and 19 miles east of Portola. It is about a 10-mile drive along Frenchman Lake Road to get to the reservoir.

Resources

Fly shops in this area include:

■ **Sportsmen's Den**, 1580 East Main Street, Quincy, CA. 95971, telephone (530) 283-2733, a full-service fly shop.

■ **Sierra Mountain Sports**, 501 Main Street, Quincy, CA 95971, telephone (530) 283-2323, which has a large fly-fishing section.

■ **The Grizzly Country Store**, Lake Davis, (530) 832-0270, and **Wiggin's Trading Post**, (530) 993-4583, located at the intersection of Highway 70 and the road to Frenchman Lake, have some fly-fishing tackle.

The Plumas County Visitor's Bureau, 550 Crescent Street, Quincy, CA 95971, telephone (800) 326-2247 or (530) 283-6345, e-mail: plumasco@psln.com, has information on lodging, camping, restaurants, and so on. So does **The Eastern Plumas Chamber of Commerce**, 73136 Highway 70, Portola, CA 96122, telephone (800) 995-6057 or (530) 832-5444, and **Plumas National Forest** headquarters, 159 Lawrence Street, Quincy, CA 95971, (530) 283-2050.

Jay Messina picked up this rainbow trolling a Woolly Bugger on Lake Davis.

Chapter 13

The Lakes Basin

GOLD LOWER SARDINE UPPER SALMON PACKER
SNAG HAVEN BIG BEAR LITTLE BEAR CUB
GRASS ROCK JAMISON WADES

There are plenty of reasons to visit the Lakes Basin in Plumas County, not far from Graeagle. More than thirty mountain lakes are nestled in spectacular Sierra scenery from 5,000 to 7,000 feet above sea level. Campgrounds abound, and there are a handful of lodges, restaurants, and motels. All in all, it is a great place for a vacation.

You'll notice I didn't single out the fishing as the big reason to go. While most of the lakes hold fish, for the most part they are planters, and with a few exceptions, this water isn't rich enough in food for them develop into the brawny holdover trout of some other areas. There are some hike-in lakes that support a wild-trout population, but generally this is family-style, put-and-take fishing. By all means go, but don't expect big, sophisticated fish.

The Lakes Basin Recreation Area is reached via Gold Lake Road, either from Highway 49 to the south or from Highway 89 near Graeagle from the north.

For all the lakes, the Sierra smorgasbord of flies is standard trout fare – Hare's Ears, Pheasant Tails, Bird's Nests, Prince Nymphs, and Zug Bugs, size 12 and 14, plus the reliable Adams, Light Cahill, and caddis imitations, size 12 to 16, and Woolly Buggers and leech patterns fished slowly and deep. Damselflies aren't as prevalent in these high lakes as in some other areas.

A Parachute Adams is a must-have fly for any angler fishing mayfly dries.

The Gold Lakes Basin has numerous beautiful waters, such as Haven Lake, but for the most part the fishing is only so-so.

Here is a rundown of the major lakes in the basin.

Gold Lake: This is the largest of the stillwaters and has rainbows, browns, and Mackinaws, some of them large. It also has a resort, campground, and a boat ramp, and as a result is a busy lake. Because it is deep, the best chance for a fly-line angler is to fish the shoreline and coves during the early morning or evening. The water is crystal-clear, and when there is no wind, which is rare, the fish will hold deep.

Lower Sardine: This easy-access lake, which has a resort, camping, and boat ramp, is worth going to just for the view. It is nestled just below the 8,587-foot-high Sierra Buttes, which form a magnificent backdrop. Use a float tube or a boat (there's a 5-mile-per-hour speed limit) and fish the edges. Upper Sardine Lake is reached along a very rocky 4x4 road that is better walked than driven – it is less than half a mile from Lower Sardine. Upper Sardine can be fished from the shore and gets less pressure.

Upper Salmon: Another lake with amenities, including a resort. However, it does not have a boat ramp, although boats can be launched from the shore. It is worm-dunker water.

Packer: Small and pretty, with a primitive campground, Packer offers nice fishing if you are willing to settle for stocked rainbows.

Snag Lake: Not many people fish Snag Lake because it is not heavily planted. That might be a plus for some anglers, because there are some large holdover rainbows here. Catching them is another matter, of course.

Haven Lake: Near Snag Lake and almost as pretty, this stillwater offers fishing for lots and lots of little brookies.

If you want to do some easy hiking, you might try Big Bear, Little Bear, and Cub Lakes on the Round Lake Trail. The trailhead is on Gold Lake Road about a mile north of the Gold Lake turnoff. It is an easy half-mile walk to Big Bear, with the other two lakes close by.

An alternative for more serious hikers is a series of lakes that are more easily reached by driving to Plumas Eureka State Park, which is off Highway 89 north of Graeagle. From the trailhead at the Upper Jamison Campground, you can hike less than 2 miles to Grass Lake and another couple of miles to Rock Lake and Jamison Lake. Wades Lake can be reached on a trail that splits off after you pass Grass Lake.

You'll find a lot of brookies in these lakes, but some are a decent size, rather than the usual high-Sierra dinks. Jamison is probably the best.

There are numerous lakes in the Lakes Basin Recreation Area, and most of them probably hold trout. I've never heard of any that are great fishing, but you never know – if you like to hike and fish, you just might find a sleeper.

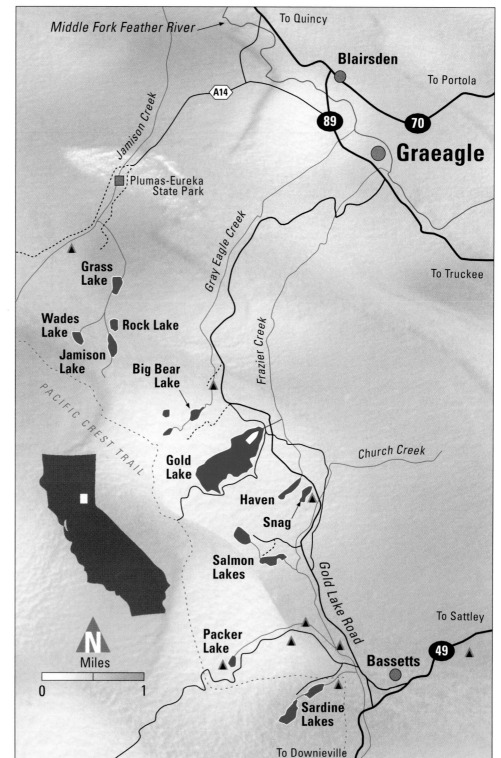

Resources

Fly shops in this area include:
■ **Nevada City Anglers**, 417 Broad Street, Nevada City, CA 95959, telephone (530) 478-9301.

■ **Sportsmen's Den**, 1580 East Main Street, Quincy, CA 95971, telephone (530) 283-2733.

■ **Sierra Mountain Sports**, 501 Main Street, Quincy, CA 95971, telephone (530) 283-2323.

The **Plumas County Visitors Bureau** offers details of camping and just about anything else you need to know about the area. It can be reached at 550 Crescent Street, Quincy, CA 95971, telephone (800) 326-2247, web site: www.plumasco@psln.com.

The **Lakes Basin Recreation Area** is in the Plumas National Forest, which can be reached at 153 Lawrence Street, Quincy, CA 95971, telephone (530) 283-2050.

Lower Sardine Lake is one of the prettiest lakes around, with a magnificent backdrop of mountains.

Packer Lake has easy access and stocked rainbows.

Chapter 14

The Truckee area

MARTIS CREEK MILTON STAMPEDE BOCA PROSSER CREEK

Truckee-area anglers are blessed with two of the top fly-fishing stillwaters in the state – Martis Creek Lake and Milton Reservoir. The catch is that the fish in these waters can be demanding, difficult, frustrating, and all the other adjectives that sometimes makes us wonder if it really is worthwhile.

In other words, this isn't toss-an-attractor water. You need to be able to match the hatch with nymphs, emergers, dries, size, color, and presentation to be successful.

One way to learn the ropes is to hire a guide for a day or two. A cheaper way is to fish with a friend who knows the area. The third way, of course, is to do it on your own – but be prepared to put in time and suffer frustration while earning your stripes.

There are numerous easier stillwater alternatives in the heavily fished Truckee area. The three largest and better-known lakes are Stampede, Boca, and Prosser Creek Reservoirs, all within a few minutes' drive of Truckee. They are big lakes that have a variety of trout, including catchable stockers, holdovers, and a few wild fish. They also are recreation lakes that have boating, sailing, swimming, and a high percentage of keep-your-catch worm dunkers.

The Martis Midge, a must for anglers on Martis Creek Lake. Note how its tail sinks.

Andy Burk, the maestro of Martis Creek Lake, demonstrates the way it should be done.

MARTIS CREEK LAKE

This seventy-acre reservoir is only a few miles from Truckee. Go south 2.5 miles on Highway 267 toward Kings Beach and the north shore of Lake Tahoe. The turnoff to Martis is just past the airport, and is clearly marked. It is about a mile to the campground, just off the road on the right. A dirt road goes from the campground to the adjoining lake.

Regulations are catch-and-release, barbless flies and lures, and although prams and float tubes are allowed, no motors of any kind are permitted. There is parking, either on a knoll overlooking the lake or at the lake itself on a small peninsula. The second is the best for putting in a pram or float tube.

Martis Creek Lake has a north-south orientation, with Martis Creek flowing in from the south and the dam at the northern end. The inlet area is shallow, and there is a

defined channel from the creek. This area is called "The Flats," and as the summer wears on, it has heavy weed growth. On the eastern side, across from the peninsula parking area, is a bay. A spring flows in at the southern end, which is fairly shallow, but the central and northern end of the bay offer deeper water and are good spots for an angler fishing from the shore.

The lake then narrows for about a hundred yards before opening out in the dam area. There is another little feeder creek to the east, not far from the dam.

There are so many hatches and different bugs, not to mention leeches and baitfish, that it is impossible to do more than generalize on what to bring as flies. I strongly recommend stopping at Truckee River Outfitters, a branch store of the Reno Fly Shop on Truckee's main drag, and talk to manager Andy Burk or one of his

knowledgeable guides about what is happening on the lake. They will possess up-to-the-minute information and they always have a selection of hot flies.

Fishing the lake with Andy Burk is an awesome experience. He is so plugged into what is going on there that he is able to anticipate what will happen next and change his fly to have it on the water when it does, while most of us mere-mortal fly fishers still are peering at the water trying to determine whether the fish are taking a nymph or an emerger.

Burk notes that one of the foods in Martis is baitfish, specifically Lahontan redsides, dace, and sunfish.

"I've caught fish on streamers from opening day until closing day," he says. "It can be a full-time deal, particularly fishing for the big browns that are looking for bait. For somebody who is willing to take fewer fish and doesn't mind doing

There is an abundance of trout in Martis Creek Lake; catching them is another matter.

depths easier – Burk says he comes prepared with several rods already rigged. And don't go long and light on the tippet – 7 feet and 10-pound test will do. Let the streamer sink until it is near the bottom and then strip like mad. It can be hard work, but the payoff could produce some spectacular browns.

At Martis, as at every lake, trolling black, brown, or olive leeches and Woolly Buggers is popular and does catch fish. But it doesn't come close to producing the numbers that can be caught by matching the hatch.

There are myriad *Callibaetis*, caddisflies, and damselflies, but the year-round main fare for the fish are chironomids, particularly Blood Midges. A fly fisher needs to have them in all stages – larva, pupa, emerger, and adult. Burk says that one trick is to fish them in an oversized pattern, a size 10 or 12. "It's strange to call a three-quarter-inch bug a midge," he says, "but it works."

a lot of casting, use a streamer in a size 6 or 8. You need something that matches the minnows in Martis, possibly yellow to imitate the sunfish, like the Stanley Streamer.

"You can't move that streamer fast enough to keep it away from the browns – they will get it! It's one of those things that can always be counted on to produce fish – although not the most fish, some of the bigger fish."

He suggests using a pontoon boat or pram, rather than a float tube, to make casting and fast stripping easier. Different shooting heads make exploring different

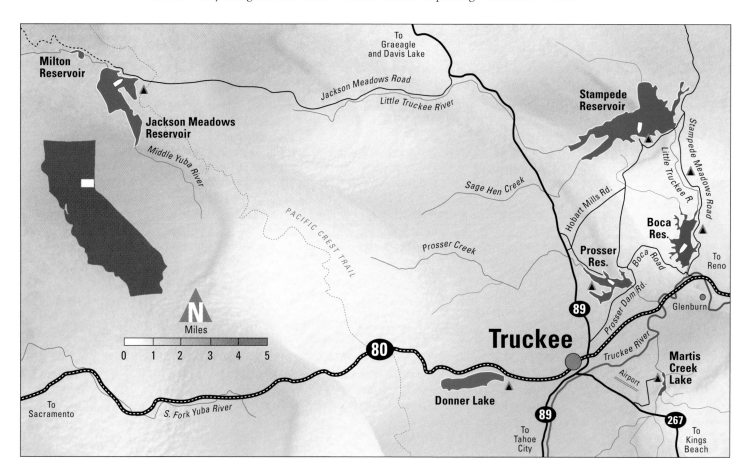

Milton Reservoir, just below Jackson Meadows Reservoir, is a first-rate fishery for fly-line anglers. It can be tough going for the novice.

MILTON RESERVOIR

Milton Reservoir is not as well known as Martis Creek Lake, but it offers fishing that is just as good and perhaps even better. That's the good news. The bad news: It's just as difficult, perhaps more so, than Martis.

To get to Milton, take Highway 89 north from Truckee (toward Quincy) for 17 miles, then turn west on Jackson Meadows Road. It is 16 miles along the paved road to Jackson Meadows Reservoir, where there is camping and a boat ramp, then another 2 miles down a dirt road to Milton. There are a few spots along the wooded bank where you can camp, but no facilities are available. There is no boat ramp, although a pram can be hand-launched at a couple of spots or a small boat can be backed in on a trailer.

Milton sits at 5,690 feet and is prettier than most mountain impoundments, with trees hugging the bank and a lush meadow (more of a bog early in the season) at the upper end where the Middle Fork of the Yuba River flows in. It is rejuvenated water – California Trout and the Department of Fish and Game poisoned it in 1981 to get rid of trash fish, mostly bullheads and golden shiners, then restocked it and let it return to a wild fishery. It was deepened in 1993, which has more clearly defined some of the main channels.

Lures and flies with barbless hooks are required, and anglers can keep two fish, twelve inches or smaller. It is worth noting that poachers make their way to the lake in winter and, fishing through the ice, take out any number of trout. Wardens in the area describe it as one of their main problems.

Milton can be fished either from the shore or with a float tube or pram, depending on where you want to fish. Where the Middle Fork of the Yuba flows in at the eastern end of the lake is a favorite place for wading anglers. You need to work your way to the creek channel, which is south of a small island near the inlet. The trick is to find where the fish are holding – usually in the channel – and then offer them something tasty.

There are several tree stumps scattered around in this area, excellent spots for holding fish. Some can be reached by wading, while for others, a float tube is best. Be cautious while wading, because there are muddy spots, holes, and sudden drop-offs.

The water gets progressively deeper toward the west, with the deepest water near the dam. Unless you want to work a limited area from the bank, a pram or float tube is necessary there.

Although the season at Milton

opens on the last Saturday in April, in reality, anglers may not be able to get to the lake until later – it depends on when the snow melts and the road is open, which often isn't until June. But when they can get in, the season is quickly off and running, with big bugs such as Woolly Buggers, leech imitations, and damselfly nymphs the flies of choice.

At this point, trout are feeding actively, coming off a hard winter, and until they bulk up, they'll make an extra effort to grab anything they think is edible. Big Gray Drake and *Callibaetis* nymphs are particularly effective, and during the first warm days, there is a "hatch" of big carpenter ants. Trout throw caution to the winds and go after them voraciously – any of the imitations will do, particularly if they float well.

There are a few Blood Midges in Milton, but not nearly as many as at Martis. However there are plenty of other members of the chironomid family, along with an abundance of Gray Drakes and *Callibaetis*. Chironomids are available to trout throughout the season and should be fished in all their stages – larva, pupa, emerger, and adult. They come in about a size 12 in the spring, but get smaller as summer wears on, becoming as tiny as size 20 or 22 in the late summer and fall.

Andy Burk describes Milton as "one of the toughest lakes to fish" and says he likes to walk the shoreline to spot big fish, particularly browns. "You may not have the chance to get to them then, but it's nice to know they are there, and you can always come back another day."

His recommendation for getting big trout in Milton is to fish chironomid imitations on a light leader, such as 6X. "The most effective colors are gray, rust, olive, orange, and black. They should be simple, with a slim body and dubbed head. You don't need a work-of-art fly – it should be skinny and easy to tie. If you are hooking big browns on light tippets you'll be losing a lot of flies. I've gone through a dozen or a dozen-and-a-half flies in a day."

STAMPEDE, BOCA, AND PROSSER CREEK RESERVOIRS

All three reservoirs are a short distance north of Truckee, have easy access, and are popular for all sorts of water sports during the summer months. They form a rough triangle, with Boca and Prosser Creek close to Interstate 80, while Stampede, the largest, is a bit farther north. Prosser is just off Highway 89, three miles north of Truckee, while Boca and Stampede are best reached via Stampede Dam Road from the Boca/Hirschdale exit off I-80. It is just a mile to Boca and another 6 miles to Stampede.

Milton Reservoir browns are big and healthy. Keep them that way by treating them gently.

Andy Burk's advice for Milton Reservoir:

"You don't need a work-of-art fly — it should be skinny and easy to tie. If you are hooking big browns on light tippets you'll be losing a lot of flies. I've gone through a dozen or a dozen-and-a-half flies in a day."

Stampede: The DFG describes this 3,400-acre lake as a "target fishery" for planting catchable-sized hatchery rainbows. Specifically, from early spring to midsummer, it dumps in about 20,000 trout big enough to keep (ten to twelve inches), along with thousands of fingerling kokanee salmon and Mackinaw trout. In addition, brown trout have been planted over the years, and there are a number of them inhabiting the reservoir that have grown to lunker size.

The Mackinaws, or lake trout, also have reached monster size, with some of them now in the ten-to-twelve-pound range. However, they usually are caught by trolling deep – it's very seldom, except in the early spring, when they come up to feed in the shallows, that a fly fisher will hook one.

Like many lakes, Stampede is open to fishing all year, but is best at ice-out, when large Woolly Buggers and streamers are effective. The best fly fishing in the spring or fall is in the shallower water on the north side of the lake, particularly in areas where there are weed beds or springs.

This reservoir is fed mainly by the Little Truckee River, which flows in from the west, and during the summer it is drawn down sharply to keep water flowing into Boca and then the main Truckee River.

There are campgrounds and a boat ramp on the southern side of Stampede.

Boca: Like Stampede, Boca is planted with catchable trout – about 11,000 a year, according to the DFG. There also are kokanee and a few Mackinaws in this 1,000-acre lake, which is 5,700 feet above sea level. At one time it was a good brown trout fishery, but there has been a steady decrease in the population of browns since the late 1990s, and there are few left in the lake.

The best fly fishing in Boca actually is just above the lake, where the Little Truckee River flows in from Stampede Reservoir to the north. It is wadable water most of the time, because the flow from Stampede is controlled. The best times to fish it are in the spring and fall, when the trout move out of the lake into shallower water. Nymphs and streamers, olive, black, or yellow, size 6 to 10, are the most effective flies.

Again, this is a popular recreation area, with a boat ramp and two campgrounds, and in reality, trolling lures or bait from a boat is the most effective fishing method in most of the lake. It is open all year and has no special restrictions.

Prosser Creek Reservoir: There are 20,000 catchable-sized trout planted here each year, along with 100,000 fingerlings. The good news is that there still is a naturally reproducing population of browns. Many local fly-line anglers consider it the best of the three reservoirs, particularly at ice-out in the spring, and again in the fall. The inlets from Prosser and Alder Creeks in the northwest part of the lake are the best areas, and streamers, Woolly Buggers, Zonkers, and Muddler Minnows are the recommended flies.

It has a 10-mile-per-hour speed limit for boats, which can help anglers who want to float tube. Facilities include a boat ramp and three campgrounds. The best place to stay is Prosser Campground, on a wooded peninsula on the southwestern end of the lake.

Resources

Fly shops in this area include:

■ **Truckee River Outfitters,** 10200 Donner Pass Road, Truckee, CA 96151, telephone (530) 582-0900, a branch of the Reno Fly Shop that is open April through October.

■ **Mountain Hardware and Sports**, 11320 Donner Pass Road, a block off I-80 at Gateway, Truckee, CA 96151, telephone (530) 587-4844, which has a good fly-fishing section.

■ **Bud's Sporting Goods**, 10108 Commercial Row, Truckee, CA 96151, (530) 587-3177, which has some fly-fishing equipment.

■ **Tahoe Fly Fishing Outfitters**, 3433 Lake Tahoe Boulevard/Highway 50, South Lake Tahoe, CA 96150, (530) 541-8208.

For information on camping contact the **Truckee Ranger District** of the U.S. Forest Service, 10342 Highway 89 North, Truckee, CA 96161, telephone (530) 478-6257.

For information on lodging, and other such matters, contact the **Truckee Chamber of Commerce**, 12036 Donner Pass Road, Truckee, CA 96161, telephone (530) 587-2757.

Chapter 15

The Markleeville area

HEENAN RED CRATER SCOTT'S INDIAN CREEK CAPLES
SILVER WOODS BURNSIDE BLUE TWIN MEADOW
TAMARACK SUMMIT HELL HOLE SUNSET RAYMOND

There are dozens of lakes – the chamber of commerce counts more than sixty – in Alpine County, on the eastern slope of the Sierra Nevada. When it comes to fly fishing, some of them are good, some are pretty good, lots are fair, but none of them rank in the excellent category unless you are a fan of Heenan Lake and its Lahontan cutthroats. Those negatives shouldn't count against fishing here, though, because atmosphere, scenery, and all the other things that go into making this sport so much fun are available.

Heenan Lake, with its restricted, catch-and-release fishing for big Lahontan cutthroat spawners, is the centerpiece for the area. It gets crowded during its short fall season – sometimes it seems like every fly-fishing club in Northern California goes there for a group fish-out.

Heenan aside, the best time for lake fishing around Markleeville is in the early summer, just after ice-out. The trout that made it through the winter are hungry, and anglers willing to brave the unpredictable weather can have multifish days on most of the lakes. Summer fishing can be slow, but then the action picks up again in the fall, when the temperatures drop, telling the fish that it is time to stock up on food before the long, hard winter begins.

Markleeville, the only community worthy of the word "town" in sparsely populated Alpine County, is a quick drive down Highway 89 from South Lake Tahoe. It also can be reached from the western side

Peter Bauer with a typical Woods Lake stocker. Woods is one of the few natural lakes in the Markleeville area.

Heenan Lake holds California's broodstock of native Lahontan cutthroat and is open for catch-and-release fishing for only a couple of months in the fall.

of the Sierra Nevada via Highway 88 from Jackson, Highway 4 from Arnold, or from the south by way of Highway 395 and Highway 89. The drive over Ebbetts Pass on Highway 4 is one of the prettiest routes across the Sierra, but be warned: It is a narrow, winding road that isn't suitable for large motor homes or long trailers. Don't try it unless you know how to handle your vehicle on mountain roads.

Markleeville is the product of a short-lived silver rush in the 1860s and doesn't flaunt the tourist-driven economy that many of the Sierra's Gold Rush towns have adopted to make their economic way in the modern world. That's a plus, as far as I'm concerned. You might not have much choice in where to stay or what to eat, but this is a town dedicated to fishing. That's what the locals do, and that is for the most part what they expect their visitors to do, too.

The Cutthroat Saloon in the center of town is the main hangout. (Don't blink, or you'll miss downtown Markleeville.) If you are uptight and politically correct, don't bother. To start with, the brassieres hanging from the ceiling along with a few other knickknacks of women's underwear might bother you. Bikers, ranging from Hell's Angels to weekend-warrior wannabes, are regular visitors, and having several dozen Harleys parked neatly along the road is not unusual.

Personally, I've had nothing but good treatment at the hands of the locals. They are friendly, happy to talk, and can be very informative about current fishing conditions. The laid-back atmosphere is conducive to schmoozing, and if you go about it right (you're on your own here), you can get an amazing amount of fishing information from folks who at first glance you wouldn't think would know a Royal Wulff from Power Bait.

What is referred to as the eastern slope of the Sierra Nevada begins in this area and stretches south to Bishop. The 430-mile-long mountain range that forms California's spine has a more gradual slope on its western side, but drops sharply along the eastern slope,

sometimes thousands of feet in a matter of miles. This rugged eastern section of the Sierra is really a high-plains desert, with more sagebrush than pine, and offers some of the prime fishing in the Golden State, although the best of it is south of the Markleeville area.

Fish are abundant because there is plenty of food for them to eat. The eastern slope is rich in minerals, which wash into the water and cause plants to flourish. They in turn support heavy concentrations of aquatic insects, the mainstay nourishment for trout. Biologists estimate that eastern-slope trout generally grow twice as fast as those in the rest of the Sierra Nevada because of the abundance of food.

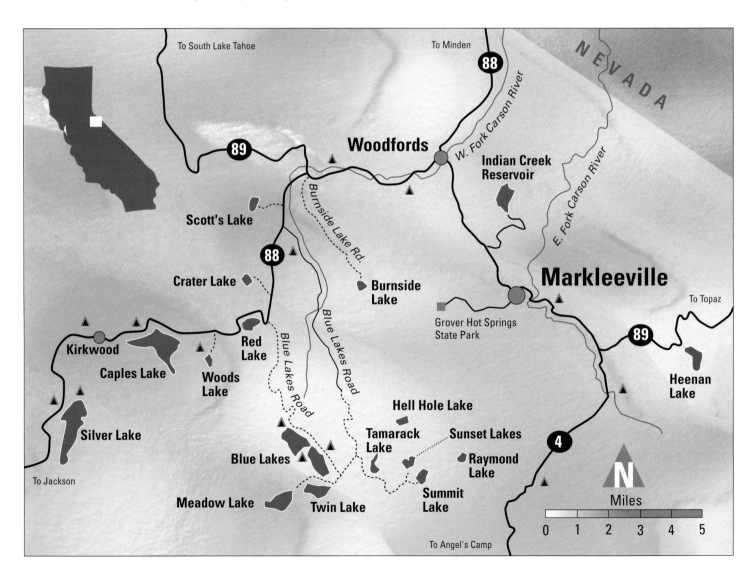

Lahontan cutthroat vary widely in color. Some are silver while others have strong colors, including the red slash along the gills that gave them their name.

HEENAN LAKE

If you never have fished Heenan, you must try it. Whether you go back ... well, that's your choice. I used to fish it regularly every fall, but now it is only an occasional destination because I'm not fond of group fishing.

Heenan was, and perhaps still is, California's best guaranteed big-fish lake, apart from those pay-to-play ponds. The 129-acre lake is the holding pen for the Lahontan cutthroats that the California Department of Fish and Game uses for spawning. There aren't many small fish in Heenan – an eighteen-incher is normal, twenty-inchers are common, and there have been fish thirty inches and longer caught. And would you believe it, a forty-four-inch female was landed in 1992. The icing on the cake: If the bite is on, anglers can have a multifish day.

Lahontan cutthroats are native trout. They inhabited prehistoric Lake Lahontan, which not long ago in geological history covered a good portion of what is now Nevada. Pyramid Lake in Nevada and Walker Lake on the California-Nevada border, today's remnants of Lake Lahontan, were filled with the cutts, including huge fish that weighed forty or fifty pounds. We took care of that shortly after the California Gold Rush simply by catching and eating them in such numbers that they could not reproduce fast enough. Now Lahontans are bred by the DFG in the Shasta and Hot Creek Hatcheries from eggs and roe taken from Heenan Lake trout and by the U.S. Fish and Wildlife Service in nearby Gardnerville, Nevada, and then planted in a number of lakes and streams, mostly in the eastern-slope area.

They often are a beautiful fish, distinguished by the red slash along the gills that is the hallmark of the cutthroat trout. In Heenan, they come in a variety of colors. Some are almost entirely silver, like steelhead, others most definitely with traditional Lahontan colors, including dark backs and a side band that is almost blood-red. For some anglers, they have two things against them. First, they aren't a particularly smart or selective fish and don't seem to learn caution by being caught on flies a number of times. Otherwise, with all the pressure they get during the brief season, fishing would become extremely difficult.

Second, and perhaps more important, Lahontans usually don't put up that much of a fight. A similar-sized rainbow will take an angler into the backing, but Lahontans for the most part do a bit of head shaking and make several short runs before coming to the net.

A good way to get the feel of Red Lake is to drive up Highway 88 toward the pass and then stop at one of the pullouts overlooking the lake. Weather and sun angle permitting, fly fishers can see the channels at the shallow, upper (western) end of the lake, away from the dam. These channels are hangout areas for fish and a favorite place for fly-line anglers.

All of which isn't to say you should skip Heenan Lake. You definitely should go there and sample these beautiful native fish.

Regulations for Heenan are complicated. From the Friday before Labor Day, it is open on Fridays, weekends, and Labor Day itself through the Sunday before (or on) October 31. Fishing is limited to catch-and-release, barbless-hooked flies and lures – no bait. Boats with electric motors are permitted on the lake, but float tubes are the most popular way to fish because there is no ramp, and boats must be small enough to be hand-launched.

Heenan is just off Highway 89, 8 miles east of Markleeville or 4.2 miles south on Highway 89 toward Monitor pass from the Highway 89 and Highway 4 intersection. There

isn't any sign, but the parking lot, often filled to overflowing, is only a couple of hundred yards from the highway and easy to spot. There is a fence around the lake and parking lot, and fishing is permitted from sunrise to sunset (signs will tell you the exact time), with no camping.

There used to be a $3.00 fee to fish the lake, which in effect paid for the DFG warden stationed there to enforce the regulations. That was dropped a few years back, but may be reinstated at some point. Enforcement varies from volunteer members of area fly-fishing clubs to visits from the warden and the on-site presence of a retired DFG warden.

The lake has a checkered history that began in 1982, when the California Wildlife Conservation

Board acquired it to use as the Lahontan cutthroat breedery. Several years later, the board opened the lake to catch-and-release fishing. For the first few years it was a well-kept secret, but those days are long gone, and it gets plenty of pressure during its September-to-October season.

There also were problems from a massive fish kill caused by a huge algae bloom that sucked the oxygen out of the water and from an over-enthusiastic drawdown of water by the Nevada rancher who owns the water rights. (Would you believe the DFG has the right to use the water, but the rancher still owns it?) Although well within his legal rights, when he realized the extent of the damage, the rancher promised to be more careful in the future

Red Lake brook trout come in a variety of sizes but many of them are in the 10-13-inch range.

Red Lake is an easy-access water off Highway 88 that is loaded with brookies eager to jump on just about any fly.

and not take so much water from Heenan, a promise that as of this writing has been kept. Despite these setbacks, Heenan's cutthroats came back strongly, and it remains a healthy and viable fishery.

As for fishing itself, dry flies are only occasionally successful, and then only early in the day or about the time of the evening you have to get off the lake. This is a Woolly Bugger, leech, nymph, and streamer place.

Back in the good old days of the '80s, when the lake originally opened to fishing, it used to be that just dragging a black, olive, or brown Woolly Bugger around usually guaranteed some action. Even then, however, I preferred to throw size 12 or 14 nymphs such as Pheasant Tails or Hare's Ears up against the bank and retrieve them very slowly. This slow retrieve with a nymph still is one of the most effective ways of fishing the lake today.

Other possibilities are suspending a nymph below an indicator and just letting it sit there at whatever depth you find most effective – usually from two to six feet – and giving it an occasional twitch. Or drop a Brassie off the nymph as a second fly – midge imitations are one of those things that can work in just about any Sierra lake. And when you can fish dries, an Adams or the like generally will do the trick, although everything from chironomids to caddis imitations will work on occasion.

Where to fish is an open question. Lahontans are pretty much everywhere, but the favorite spot is around the mouth of Heenan Creek, which feeds the lake from the east (the parking lot and put-in are at the north end of the lake). There can be a heavy weed growth in these shallow waters, and the fish cruise the edges, looking for food. A nymph tossed up against the weeds

and stripped slowly can be extremely effective. Of course, you may find yourself jockeying for position with thirty other anglers in the same area, not all of them willing to observe etiquette and leave enough space for others to fish.

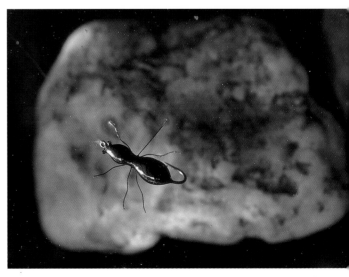

A Jeff Yamagata-tied ant imitation too perfect to waste on a fish.

Bill Sunderland probes the water at Scott's Lake.

The shallow southern end of the lake also sometimes has reeds growing and is usually good, as is the point on the west bank. I've always believed that a lot of the bigger fish hang out near the dam at the north end, not far from where the parking lot is located. But they usually are a bit deeper and thus harder to reach.

For the most part, a sink-tip or slow-sinking line works well, putting the fly a few feet under the surface. Occasionally, for example when fishing near the dam at midday, you'll need added weight or a quick-sinking line. And if you're going to try dries early or late, a floating line is necessary.

While float tubes or prams are the most popular way to fish, Heenan also can be effectively fished from the bank, and plenty of fly and spin anglers just walk around the sides. For the most part,

it is pretty much open, so casting isn't a problem from shore.

RED LAKE

Red Lake is probably the best of the many easy-access lakes in the Markleeville area. It lies alongside Highway 88 near Carson Pass, a long, fairly shallow lake that is about 8,200 feet above sea level and is noted mostly for its brookies. It is equidistant from South Lake Tahoe and from Markleeville, both about thirty to thirty-five minutes away.

A good way to get the feel of Red Lake is to drive up Highway 88 toward the pass and then stop at one of the pullouts overlooking the lake. Weather and sun angle permitting, fly fishers can see the channels at the shallow, upper (western) end of the lake, away from the dam. These channels are hangout areas for fish and a favorite place for fly-line anglers.

There is no boat ramp at Red Lake, but small boats can be put in from the north side, reached by a short, unmarked dirt road off Highway 88. The main, paved road to Red Lake is marked and dead-ends at a parking area on the lake less than half a mile from Highway 88. For float tubers, it is a long kick to the upper end of the lake. An easier way is to haul your gear along the bank for several hundred yards before putting in.

While the upper end of the lake generally is considered to offer the best fly fishing, the lower end at the dam is deeper and usually holds bigger trout. But getting them, particularly during hot summer days, can be more difficult because they hold deeper. However, they do come up in the evening for caddisflies and mayfly dries, and fishing Red Lake at dusk can be a blast.

The best advice here is don't

The best advice here is don't expect to catch big fish — and be pleasantly surprised if you pick up a lunker. In fact, there are big browns, brookies, and rainbows in Red Lake, most of which were put in as fingerlings and have survived to become "wild" trout. There also are some Lahontan cutthroats, which are occasionally transplanted from Heenan Lake.

expect to catch big fish – and be pleasantly surprised if you pick up a lunker. In fact, there are big browns, brookies, and rainbows in Red Lake, most of which were put in as fingerlings and have survived to become "wild" trout. There also are some Lahontan cutthroats, which are occasionally transplanted from Heenan Lake.

The usual catch, however, consists of small brookies in the six-to-ten-inch range. They can be caught just about anyplace, particularly by casting dries up against the shore. For bigger fish, go deeper with a full-sinking or sink-tip line. Flies favored by locals are black or brown Woolly Buggers and Antron Caterpillars. There also are scuds in the lake, so give those a try, too. For dries, a Pale Morning Dun or Light Cahill, size 12 to 16, will work early in the day, and in the evening, caddis imitations in about the same sizes can be effective.

Like most other lakes in this area, Red Lake is best fished as soon as possible after ice-out and then again in the fall, when the temperature drops and the fish begin beefing up for winter. Summer can be slow, unless you are satisfied with the small brook trout that will jump on just about anything you want to toss at them.

CRATER LAKE AND SCOTT'S LAKE

Crater is a lovely alpine lake that is 2.1 miles off Highway 88 on a dirt road. A 4x4 is needed to make it all the way to the lake, but an alternative is to drive as far as you can in your trusty sedan and then hike the last half-mile or so to the lake.

The good news is that there are lots of brookies in Crater Lake. The bad news is that not many of them are very big. I singled it out because it is so pretty, and I've always caught fish there, even if they are small brook trout. Besides, it doesn't get much pressure, and it is fun paddling around with nobody else in sight.

Although you can fish from the bank, a float tube gives you much more maneuverability. The standard Sierra flies work – Prince Nymphs, Zug Bugs, and Bird's Nests, size 12 to 16, or attractors in about the same sizes. Match the hatch if you will, but in most cases, it isn't really necessary.

The turnoff to Crater Lake is to the west from Highway 88, 5 miles after the Highway 88/89 junction.

Scott's Lake is a nearby alternative, without the need for four-wheel drive. The turnoff is north off Highway 88, 1.5 miles from the Highway 88/89 intersection. The 2.8 miles to the lake, along Forest Service Road 079A, can be done in any vehicle, although you'll need to ease over a few rough spots.

Again, you'll find lots of brookies. This lake is shallower than Crater, and access along the shore is a bit more difficult. The deeper water is near the dam, an area that can be fished from shore, but the fish can be anywhere.

THE BEST OF THE REST

Indian Creek Reservoir: This large reservoir has had its ups and downs – some folks love it and do well there, while others use the stock phrase, "It used to be pretty good." It is 5 miles along Airport Boulevard, which branches east off Highway 89 a few miles north of Markleeville. There is a nice campground, along with a boat ramp, so it gets its share of traffic.

Jim Crouse of Alpine Anglers, who has guided in this area for years, says success on the reservoir "varies from year to year. There are now a lot of suckers, but some of the planted fish hold over and grow up to eleven pounds. The county also puts in some trophy fish. I've

Crater Lake requires a four-wheel drive. The scenery is worth the effort, even if the brookies are small.

Peter Bauer tries his hand on Blue Lake, one of a series of lakes easily accessible from Highway 88.

caught brookies, browns, and rainbows, but it is predominately a rainbow fishery.

"There's no particular area for fly fishing, although in the fall, fish are in the shallows. Since the water is fairly warm then, they'll hold in the channels." Crouse suggests using damsels, *Callibaetis* imitations, Blood Midges, Woolly Buggers, and scuds.

Caples Lake and Silver Lake: These both lie adjacent to Highway 88 on the western side of Carson Pass. Since they are easy to get to, are heavily stocked, and have no spe-

cial regulations, they are popular spots for all types of anglers. They also are fairly large lakes, easier handled in a boat than in a float tube.

Both are popular camping and boating areas, with ramps, boat rentals, and all the amenities. Both are best at ice-out, but since they are high in the Sierra (Caples is almost 8,000 feet high, and Silver is at 7,200 feet), weather can be dicey in the spring. Wind is a problem, and a calm day is a blessing for fly-line anglers. Caples covers some 600 acres, while Silver is a bit smaller. The best dry-fly fishing on Caples is

in the morning or evenings near the two dams and near the inlet at the eastern end of the lake.

Caples also offers a rarity for fly-line anglers – a chance to catch lake trout. Just after ice-out, these deep-holding fish can be found by float tubers using olive Woolly Buggers and olive Matukas on a full-sinking line. The trick is to dredge the bottom just east of the spillway.

Silver Lake also fishes best early in the season, wherever water is running into the lake. Crystal Woolly Buggers are the favored fly here, and larger trout can be caught

rainbows. In other words, go for the scenery, not for fantastic fishing.

Another natural lake is Burnside Lake, which can be reached from a dirt road that goes south from the Highway 88/89 junction. Fishing is pretty much the same as at any of the other lakes.

The road to Blue Lakes actually offers access to a variety of lakes, including Upper and Lower Blue Lakes, Twin Lake, Meadow Lake, Tamarack Lake, Summit Lake, Hell Hole, Upper and Lower Sunset Lakes, and Raymond Lake. Raymond Lake, which is a tough four-and-a-half mile hike, is worth mentioning because it holds golden trout, a prized fish in the northern part of the Sierra Nevada. The trail to Raymond Lake leaves from Wet Meadows Reservoir (no fishing allowed), which is near Summit Lake. Raymond hovers at 9,600 feet and plays host to a swirling wind, which can make fly fishing interesting. Ice-out about mid-July is the best time to fish there.

The other lakes also have plenty of trout, although not many of the fish are very large. But you never know – a four-pound brook trout was pulled out of Lower Sunset a couple of years ago.

The first 6 miles of the road to Blue Lake, which turns south from Highway 88 a couple of miles from the Highway 88/89 intersection, is paved, and then the road becomes gravel. It splits after about 10 miles, with the right fork going to Upper and Lower Blue lakes and Twin Lake, and the left fork going to Tamarack, Summit, Hell Hole, and Upper and Lower Sunset Lakes.

For the fly fisher, Lower Blue Lake is probably the best bet, although all these lakes are stocked. Fishing is best in the evening at the rock wall, and since the fish come right up to the wall, fishing from shore is possible. Try a Parachute Adams or Elk Hair Caddis, size 14 or 16.

There are plenty of other lakes in the Markleeville area, almost all of which hold fish. If you are a backpacking angler, this is a great place to explore, with myriad lakes available within a day's walk.

because this lake seems to have a good holdover base.

One of the few natural lakes in this area is Woods Lake, which can be reached via a road that turns south from Highway 88 west of Carson Pass. It is only 2 miles to the lake, and the road is paved, but the tight turns make it inadvisable for an RV or trailer. This is a developed area with a nice campground, and at 8,200 feet offers a beautiful setting against the surrounding mountains. As for fishing, there are the usual brookies, along with planted

Resources

Fly shops in this area include:
- **Angler's Edge**, 1420A Highway 395, Gardnerville, NV 89410, telephone (775) 782-4734.
- **Alpine Fly Fishing**, Grover's Corner, Markleeville, CA 96120, telephone (530) 542-0759 or (530) 694-2562.
- **Tahoe Fly Fishing Outfitters**, 3433 Lake Tahoe Boulevard/Highway 50, South Lake Tahoe, CA 96150, (530) 541-8208.
- The **Alpine County Visitor's Information Bureau** offers details of camping and just about anything else you need to know about the area. It can be reached at 3 Webster Street, Markleeville, CA 96120, telephone (530) 694-2475, fax, (530) 694-2478, e-mail, alpcnty@telis.org.

Chapter 16

The Bridgeport area

BRIDGEPORT KIRMAN ROOSEVELT LANE POORE
TWIN VIRGINIA TRUMBELL

The area around Bridgeport, on the eastern slope of the Sierra Nevada, is noted for its trout fishing, both for blue-ribbon fly-line angling and for a variety of put-and-take waters. This chapter tells you about the best of the easy-access stillwaters, but if you are a serious hiker or backpacker, the variety of lakes that offer good fishing is almost overwhelming.

Bridgeport Reservoir, just north of the little town that sits astride Highway 395, tops the list – it has some big fish lurking in its waters. We're talking trout that can weigh into the double digits. Because there are no special regulations for fishing the reservoir, some of them end up on display in an outdoor freezer with a glass top in front of Ken's Sporting Goods on Bridgeport's Main Street.

Then there's Kirman Lake, one of my personal favorites. This is a walk-in water, about an hour's easy hike along a dirt road. Again, big trout are the attraction, in this case, brookies. Yeah, I know – most of us have an image of pretty little eight-inch or nine-inch fish when we talk about brook trout. But not at Kirman. It is home to brook trout in the range of four to five pounds, trout that grow so fast they feature oversized bodies with undersized heads.

Two catch-and-release lakes, Roosevelt Lake and Lane Lake, also are a fairly easy hike.

A hook-jawed male 'bow in spawning colors.

For drive-up fishing, if you don't mind stocked trout, there are numerous choices, including Twin Lakes, Virginia Lakes, and Trumbell Lake. Most of these are better waters for bait-and-lure anglers, but they can be productive – and fun – for fly fishing at the right time. In other words, hit them in the spring or the fall, or fish them in the early morning and late evening during the summer.

Bridgeport Reservoir holds huge trout. Fly fishers need to pick the time and place to fish it, with emphasis on the spring and fall months.

BRIDGEPORT RESERVOIR

The most amazing thing about Bridgeport Reservoir is that few fly-line anglers take advantage of what it has to offer. It is a large reservoir, 4,400 surface acres when full. It sits just north of the town of Bridgeport and is easily accessed from Highway 182, which runs along the eastern edge of the teardrop-shaped impoundment.

There are three boat ramps and a marina, and there's camping on the eastern shore. There are no restrictions on the lake for fishing or for boating, although tributaries have size and take limits.

The main source of water is the East Walker River, which comes in at the larger southern end and then runs out at the narrow dam block-ing the northern end. The East Walker from the dam 7 miles to the Nevada border is one of California's premier trout streams and is the area pounded by most fly fishers visiting Bridgeport.

Where and how to fly fish the reservoir depends on the time of year. You can skip winter – although open to fishing, it sits at 6,500 feet on the frigid, unprotected eastern slope of the Sierra Nevada.

During the spring, the bay at the southern end where the East Walker River flows in holds big rainbows that are headed up the river to spawn. Access from Highway 182 is easy for float tubers. Other spots that are productive for big fish are the inlets from Robinson and Buckeye Creeks, which also are spawning streams for the lake. They're at the southwestern end of the lake and harder to reach than the Walker inlet. It is a long kick across by float tube, so making the trip by boat – even if you use a float tube once you get there – will save a lot of energy. Besides, the wind can pick up in a hurry and make float tubing back across the lake difficult, or even dangerous.

Keep in mind that these areas also will be hot spots during the fall, when the browns are staging in preparation for spawning runs.

As spring and summer come on, weed growth proliferates in Bridgeport Reservoir, which is quite shallow, except for the area near the dam. Although the fish are feeding throughout most of the lake, the heavy weed growth and algae bloom makes fly-line angling difficult, although it can be done by determined anglers.

Otherwise, the best place is near the dam, where the water is about forty feet deep. Big fish, particularly browns, hold among the rocks, and if you can get down to them with a streamer or other morsel, particu-larly at daybreak or when it is getting dark, they can be caught.

There is a proliferation of insects and other fish food in Bridgeport Reservoir. It is much the same as in the better-known Crowley Lake to the south – mayflies, caddisflies, damselflies, scuds, snails, and leeches. Bridgeport also has Sacramento perch, a favorite trout delicacy, but not in the same huge quantities as Crowley. Still, a perch fry imitation should be part of your arsenal any time from July on and should be fished along the edges of weed beds. Hornberg Specials or Spruce Matukas are the local favorites.

Olive, brown, and black Woolly Buggers and leech patterns are a

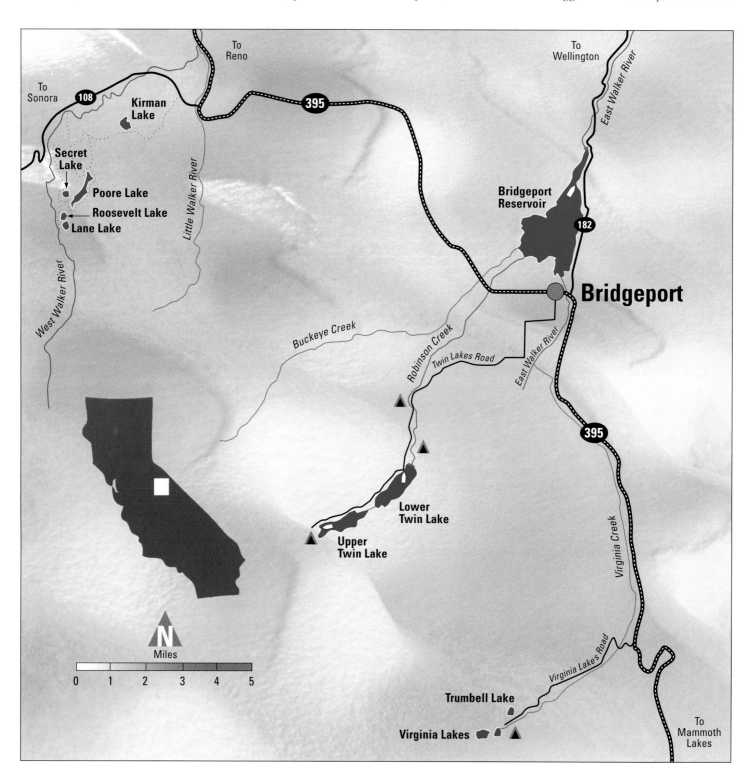

Kurt Krug effectively fishes Kirman Lake from the shore, although most anglers use float tubes.

must, size 4 to 8. Otherwise, fish Bird's Nests, Zug Bugs, Hare's Ears, Pheasant Tails, and Prince Nymphs, size 12 or 14. If there is a hatch on, and you see fish rising, any of the standard mayfly or caddis patterns will work. The fish here really don't see enough artificials to be shy about taking them. They aren't leader-shy, either, so go heavy enough to deal with big fish.

Bridgeport exists today as an excellent fishery, despite the Nevada ranchers who own the water, thanks to Rick Rockel, the former owner of Ken's Sporting Goods. The crunch came during the 1988-89 drought, when the ranchers emptied the reservoir, killing the trout and sluicing sediment into the prime East Walker fishery below the dam, all but wiping it out.

Rockel and CalTrout filed criminal charges against the Walker River Irrigation District in Nevada, which was fined nearly two million dollars. Even more important, they were ordered to maintain a thirty-cubic-feet-per-second flow into the East Walker River and to keep at least 500 acre-feet of water in Bridgeport Reservoir. It took a few years, but the comeback is complete, and these fisheries are as good as they have ever been.

KIRMAN LAKE

This little hike-in lake not far from the intersection of Highways 108 and 395 holds a special place in California fishing – it is the home of some of the biggest brook trout you can catch in the state. It can be unpredictable, with times when

twenty-fish days are easy to come by and other periods when anglers swear there isn't a fish in the water.

Access is off Highway 108 about half a mile west of where it intersects with Highway 395. Just across a cattle guard, there are wide spaces on both sides of the road that allow room for a dozen or so cars to park. Anglers must climb over a primitive metal stile spanning a barbed-wire fence, walk a few hundred yards along a path, climb over another stile, and then follow a dirt road to the lake. This is private ranch land, with plenty of cattle grazing in the area, so leave it as clean as you found it. Let the cattle do the dirtying.

It isn't a difficult walk. The road has an elevation gain of a couple of hundred feet on the way in, but

Kirman's fish, both brook trout and Lahontan cutthroats from Heenan Lake, grow exceptionally fast. A four-year-old brookie can be twenty inches long and weigh four pounds. Many of them are football-shaped, the result of their rapid growth.

there are no serious grades. It is about 3 miles to the lake – an hour or so for the average hiker. A mountain bike is ideal transportation here and can cut the time by two-thirds.

The ringer is that most of the time, fly-fishers will want to haul along a float tube because that is by far the most effective way to fish Kirman, which also is known as Carmen Lake on some old maps. Reeds choke almost all the banks along the lake, making it extremely difficult for an angler to get into position to cast. Open areas and

slots through the reeds tend to be shallow and generally unfit for fly fishing.

However, there are times when the lake level drops in the summer. During that period, anglers sometimes can wade out through the reeds on the upper end of the lake where a little creek feeds in and work flies along the edge of the growth where the fish often hang out. It's tough going, with deep muck and well-disguised holes deep enough to leave your hat floating on the water – an amusing spectator

sport, perhaps, but hard work for the person trying to get into position to fish.

Kirman was a reasonably well-kept secret for years, with no special regulations, and was fished mostly by local bait-and-lure anglers who kept their limit of fish (or more). In 1990, the Department of Fish and Game instituted special regulations, banning bait and restricting anglers to flies and lures with barbless hooks. The limit was reduced to two fish of sixteen inches or longer.

The fish here, both brook trout

This Extended Body Scud is a top-of-the line imitation of a favorite trout food.

Kirman Lake, a hike-in water, has some of the biggest brook trout in California. They often are in the four-pound class.

and Lahontan cutthroats from Heenan Lake, grow exceptionally fast. A four-year-old brookie can be twenty inches long and weigh four pounds. Many of them are football-shaped, the result of their rapid growth.

Like many eastern-slope Sierra streams and lakes, Kirman is nutrient-rich, and as a result offers a plethora of food for the trout, particularly scuds. The fish just cruise around and slurp them up, growing and growing and growing.

The problem with fishing scuds in Kirman is that there are so many naturals, it is hard to get a fish to take an artificial. I've usually had better luck fishing size 12 to 14 dark nymphs, although damselfly imitations or olive or black Woolly Buggers also work well. Dries don't seem to be much use here, although if somebody is around in the evening (which few people are, since there is no place to camp), they might be more effective.

ROOSEVELT LAKE AND LANE LAKE

Roosevelt and Lane Lakes are side-by-side waters that are part of a series of hike-in lakes nestled above the Leavitt Meadows area south of Highway 108. They are in the state Catch-and-Release Program, with a two-trout limit, but fishing in the other lakes in the same area is just as good. Poore Lake, in particular, has brookies almost as big as Kirman's.

To get to any of the lakes, go west on Highway 108 from Highway 395 toward Sonora Pass. Leavitt Meadows, past the Marine Corps Training Camp and on the opposite side of the road, is the trailhead. Lane and Roosevelt Lakes are near the West Walker River, while Poore Lake is to the east. Other lakes worth trying if you want to do some hiking are Secret and Hidden Lakes.

Most of these lakes can be reached with an hour to an hour and a half of hiking. The trails are kept in good shape and are not too difficult.

Resources

There are no fly-fishing stores in Bridgeport, but **Ken's Sporting Goods** has a fly-fishing section that should take care of your needs. It is on Main Street, and the telephone number is (760) 932-7707. They also are happy to tell you about the latest conditions.

The town of Mammoth Lakes to the south has more choice, with a variety of fly-fishing shops and sporting-goods stores. They include:

■ **The Trout Fitter**, Shell Mart Center, Highway 203 and Old Mammoth Road, Mammoth Lakes, CA 93546, telephone (760) 924-3676, web site: www.thetroutfitter.com.

■ **The Trout Fly**, Gateway Center, Mammoth Lakes, CA 93546, telephone (760) 934-2157, web site: www.thetroutfly.com, e-mail: troutinfo@aol.com.

■ **Kittredge Sports**, Highway 203 and Forest Trail, Mammoth Lakes, CA 93546, telephone (760) 934-7566.

■ **Rick's Sports Center**, Highway 203 and Center Street, Mammoth Lakes, CA 93546, telephone (760) 934-3416.

For information on lodging and restaurants, there is **The Bridgeport Chamber of Commerce**, P.O. Box 541, Bridgeport, CA 93517, telephone (760) 932-7500, and for camping, the **U.S. Forest Service Ranger Station**, P.O. Box 595, Bridgeport, CA 93517, telephone (760) 932-7070.

Chapter 17

The Mammoth Lakes area

CROWLEY PLEASANT VALLEY LAUREL McLEOD
TWIN MARY GEORGE CRYSTAL T.J.
MAMIE HORSESHOE COTTONWOOD

Crowley Lake gets most of the ink when it comes to stillwater fishing in the Mammoth Lakes/Bishop area. Rightly so, but there are some good alternatives, even though they don't pump out those monster trout for which Crowley is noted.

Pleasant Valley Reservoir, just north of Bishop, which like Crowley is fed with water from the Owens River, is a fun alternative and not nearly as crowded. The drawback is that it is more of a put-and-take fishery, with only a few big holdovers, while Crowley is very much a put-and-grow fishery specializing in trout that have been hanging around for years.

If you enjoy high-mountain lakes and have a high-center, four-wheel-drive vehicle, work your way up to Laurel Lakes, two side-by-side special-regulations stillwaters at the 10,000-foot level that offer golden trout. There's even Lake McLeod, just outside the town of Mammoth Lakes, a zero-take fishery with lots of Lahontan cutthroats.

Other special-regulations lakes are four of the six Cottonwood Lakes near Mount Whitney, the highest mountain in the contiguous forty-eight states. They are used as a spawning area for golden trout and have a zero-keep limit. They are a tough hike in of about 5 miles. Those who want to expend less energy and don't mind catching stocked rainbows alongside worm dunkers and hardware slingers can drive up to any of a half-dozen lakes near Mammoth Lakes, including Mamie, George, Horseshoe, Mary, and Twin Lakes.

Crowley Lake has plenty of rainbows and browns, some of them planters or holdovers and others that are wild, spawned in the Owens River.

Crowley Lake is one of California's top stillwaters. September and October are the best times for big fish.

CROWLEY LAKE

Crowley, which sits at 6,720 feet and is between Mammoth Lakes and Bishop, just east of Highway 395, is a prime water, one of the best trout-fishing stillwaters in California. This isn't exactly a secret, as you'll find out when you fish it. On the other hand, it covers 650 surface acres, enough territory so that there's plenty of room for everybody.

Of course, there are well-known hot spots where there are so many float tubes that they look like Cheerios in a bowl of milk, but in reality, there are many other areas that have their share of fish and less than their share of fly fishers.

Crowley isn't open to fishing all year, as many lakes are, and it has two seasons. From the opening on the last Saturday in April through July 31, there are no special regs – you can use bait or lures and keep five fish. But from August 1 until it closes on October 31 (the eastern-slope trout-fishing season closes fifteen days before the trout closure in the rest of California), Crowley regulations are barbless flies and lures, no bait, and a two-trout limit of fish eighteen inches or larger. It is during this period, particularly in September and October, when fly fishing is the best.

Fishing Crowley really isn't that tough – you don't have to play match the hatch with educated trout, as is necessary on some smaller California stillwaters. But you certainly will catch more fish by offering them the special of the day at the right time of year in the right place.

There are both rainbows and browns in Crowley. They are planted, for the most part, but there is spawning upstream, in the Owens River, by both the browns and the rainbows. For the record, there are both spring and fall spawning runs by rainbows, with the browns doing their usual fall spawning. Both species get big – a twenty-six-pound brown is the lake record, and just about everybody who fishes Crowley regularly has had heavy tackle snapped by an unseen fish.

Although the DFG plants trout, and some are caught right away, many of them grow for years to provide fish of a size that has made the lake famous. Food is plentiful. As usual, caddisflies, mayflies, midges, damselflies, and dragonflies are common, as are snails and leeches. There's another important food source you'll need to imitate – perch fry. Along about July, Sacramento perch hatch, and the fry hang out around the numerous weed beds. Trout love 'em, and every fly box should hold some imitations. A local favorite is the Hornberg

A perch pattern is a favorite fly for catching big trout on Crowley Lake.

Special, an Eastern fly that isn't seen much in the West.

Adult perch get big, up to a couple of pounds, and are excellent eating. When they are spawning in shallow water in May and June, fly-line anglers can have a blast catching them for dinner – there's no limit. Just remember that the dorsal fins have spines, and if you attach a stringer to your tube, do it in such a way that the spines don't puncture the bladder.

As for when to fish Crowley, most fly-line types tend to do it after the special season begins, with particular emphasis in the fall from about mid-September until closing. Many locals feel this is a mistake, and that if you know where to go, it fishes well all the time.

When the season opens in April, the best area is near the mouth of the Owens River, where it runs into the lake from the north. It helps that this area is shallow, so boaters and jet skiers tend to stay away. There is no speed limit on Crowley, and there are all sorts of watercraft around during the summer. Any float tuber knows what that means – watch out!

During the hot summer months, the fish still are there, but tend to come into shallower water early or late in the day, spending the hot hours holding deep. During this period, shoreline weed beds proliferate, as do the insects, so this is the beginning of the period when big trout cruise along these beds, slurping up whatever moves. Anglers should work the edges of the beds, preferably from float tubes or pontoon boats.

Put yourself in a position where you can work your fly as close to the weeds as possible, or even in open areas in the weed beds. Just make certain you have a leader of 6 pounds test or more, because the strikes usually are vicious, and anything lighter is a waste of time and tackle. By August, the fry are on the move. Use a perch imitation, a Muddler Minnow, Matuka, or other streamer, all size 4 or 6. Make long enough casts so that you don't scare the fish. The water usually is clear at

Pleasant Valley Reservoir near Bishop is a late-comer for fly fishers, having recently been opened to float tubers.

this time of year, and the trout make a quick exit if they sense danger.

From then on, it just gets better as the perch fry grow and the fish continue to gorge themselves. The next change begins sometime in late September or early October, depending on the weather, when the weed beds die out and the trout begin to scatter. As the season draws to an end, they aren't as concentrated, but they still are around – and as the water temperature drops, they feed heavily to get ready for winter.

In addition, the browns and fall-spawning rainbows move to the northern end of the lake and into the Owens River to begin the run upriver. They also spawn in a series of creeks along the western shore, so don't neglect to fish those areas, too.

For anglers who use a boat, the only ramp is at the southwestern end of the lake. There's a clearly marked turnoff from Highway 395 to the ramp.

If you want to use a float tube or pontoon boat, which are the best ways to fly fish the lake, there are numerous put-ins. The best fly fishing is in the narrower northern half of the teardrop-shaped lake, and there is access to most of both sides.

The turnoff to the lake is east from Highway 395, just south of the Mammoth-June Lake Airport. The easily visible Green Church marks the road, which is called Benton Crossing Road. There are several dirt road turnoffs to the south from Benton Crossing Road, and these in turn split several times as they lead toward the lake. Just about any of them will take you to some point on

the lake where you can park close enough to the water to put in easily, but to go to specific areas, here are the general directions. Most lakeside areas are from 1.5 to 2 miles from the turnoff.

The first turnoff just past the Green Church doesn't go to the lake. The second turnoff at Whitmore Hot Springs leads to several bankside put-ins. Stay right, and you'll end up in the Stormy Flats / Sandy Point area. Stay left, and you'll end up at Green Banks, which is the best-known and most popular float-tubing area on Crowley. The third turnoff leads to the West Flats and the upper end of Green Banks.

To get to the eastern shore, follow Benton Crossing Road, which crosses the Owens River at the northern end of Crowley. Just after the crossing, a dirt road goes south and follows the eastern shoreline for several miles. It leads to the East Flats, Weed Point, Windy Beach, and ends at Leighton Springs. South of Leighton Springs is Alligator Point, which is a good place to fish on windy days. Stay north of the point, and if the wind blows from its usual direction, you'll have a bit of protection.

And speaking of wind ... Crowley has plenty of it. Mornings tend to be calm, but about noon, it picks up, and calm waters can quickly turn to whitecaps. Be careful – you need to be able to get back to your starting point in a hurry once the wind starts. This is a big lake, and it can be dangerous.

PLEASANT VALLEY RESERVOIR

Pleasant Valley Reservoir is a recent addition to the fly fisher's list of stillwaters. Although it has been around for a while, it wasn't until December 1998 that it was opened to float tubing, which made it viable for fly-line anglers. Getting there involves a brief walk along a paved road that is closed to vehicular traffic.

The Department of Fish and Game uses it as a put-and-take fishery, open to the public all year and with no special regulations. If they ever tighten the rules, it might produce much bigger fish.

Still, it does offer some fun fishing during the winter, when Crowley is closed. And in the fall, when storms can make Crowley unfishable, Pleasant Valley may be the ticket – it is a couple of thousand feet lower in altitude (4,200 feet as opposed to Crowley's 6,720 feet) and much more protected from the wind. It also is narrow, so wind generally doesn't sweep across a broad enough expanse to build up whitecaps.

Pleasant Valley is fed by the Owens River, as is Crowley. The water leaves Crowley through penstocks that carry it to generating plants to produce electricity, although some of it now flows into the Owens River Gorge because of a broken penstock. Just above Pleasant Valley, there is a Los Angeles Power and Water generating plant, and the water flows into Pleasant Valley from there. The flow depends on how much electricity is being generated. The Owens flows out of Pleasant Valley and into another prime fishery, the wild-trout section of the lower Owens River.

Here's the drill on getting to Pleasant Valley. There are two ways in, at the dam to the south and at the power plant on the northern end. The northern end offers the best fly-line angling. To get there,

There are brown trout in Pleasant Valley Reservoir. Locals claim there are some big ones, although not many have been caught.

Pleasant Valley Reservoir is in a narrow gorge, its rock-strewn slopes steep and difficult. That means clambering from the access road down the thirty feet or so to the water is difficult and dangerous. That is why the float-tube launch ramps were built, and anglers should use those put-ins and not try to freelance a way to the water.

turn east from Highway 395 onto Gorge Road. There is no sign, but it is about 12 miles north of Bishop and is opposite Paradise Swale Road to the west.

At a T in the road, turn right, and follow it to the power plant. There is a small parking area in front of the plant, and from there, anglers must walk across a bridge and along the paved road that follows the eastern shore of the lake. It isn't far to the first put-in, about a quarter of a mile.

To get to the lower end of the lake, turn east off Highway 395 onto Pleasant Valley Dam Road about 6 miles north of Bishop. There is parking near the dam, and you can carry a float tube and other gear up to the water. The walk is not quite as far as at the northern end, but the fishing is not as good.

Gary Gunsolley, owner of Brock's Fly Fishing Specialties in Bishop, is the person responsible for opening Pleasant Valley Reservoir to float tubers. He was able to work out an agreement with Los Angeles Power and Water and then make arrangements to have volunteer labor, in this case, convicts from a nearby prison, put in ramps that give float tubers access to the water. He also raised funds through donations for a buoy system that marks the boundary 400 feet upstream from the dam. No float tubing is allowed within that 400 feet, although anglers can fish from the bank. Only float tubes and kick boats are allowed – no rubber rafts.

Pleasant Valley Reservoir is in a narrow gorge, its rock-strewn slopes steep and difficult. That means clambering from the access road

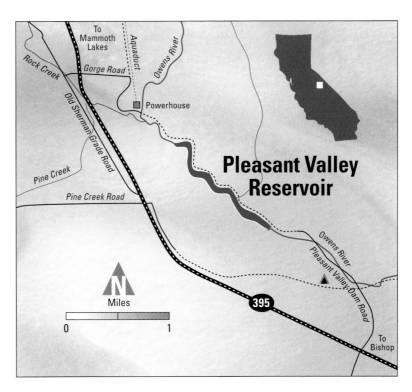

down the thirty feet or so to the water is difficult and dangerous. That is why the float-tube launch ramps were built, and anglers should use those put-ins and not try to freelance a way to the water.

Gunsolley says, "I usually put in at the first access [at the northern end], where the river widens out, but is still moving, particularly when the reservoir is low. There actually is current through the whole reservoir, even up to the dam." He uses mostly streamers and nymphs, including perch imitations.

The DFG stocks the reservoir with rainbows, including Eagle Lake strain fish, and browns. Gunsolley says that when it opened to float tubing, many local anglers thought that somebody would catch a huge

brown, perhaps a state record, but so far it has not happened. Most browns caught are in the seventeen-to-eighteen-inch range.

The reservoir is three miles long and not more than 100 or 150 yards wide in most places. There is almost no vegetation on the rocky banks, except at the upper end, where there are a few trees and weed beds.

Gunsolley notes that at the northern end, there is a short river section running from the power plant to the reservoir. The banks are lined with willows, and there is little access, so an angler once in the water has to do a lot of wading. This area can be dangerous, he says, because the water level from the power plant can increase sharply without warning, and an angler can be trapped in quickly rising water.

For golden trout, anglers can drive to Upper and Lower Laurel Lakes, although it requires a four-wheel drive with high clearance.

LAUREL LAKES

Looking for golden trout? Well, this is one of the few places you can drive to and catch them. But what a drive!

The road from Highway 395 just south of the Mammoth Lakes turnoff claws its way up the steep eastern slope of the Sierra Nevada, crossing rock-strewn stretches that have you looking nervously up at cliffs, hoping that nothing breaks loose while you are passing by. It is definitely four-wheel-drive, high-center country, and if you just bought a fancy new SUV and are eager for a chance to try it, go somewhere else where the off-roading is easier.

The turnoff to the west from Highway 395 is 1.5 miles south of the Mammoth Lakes turnoff and is marked as Sherwin Creek Road. Follow it for another mile and a half, then turn left where a sign says "Laurel Lakes, 4.5 miles."

Golden trout fry are planted from air drops into the two lakes, which sit side by side in a bowl. They grow quickly, even at the 10,000-foot altitude, mainly because of a heavy population of scuds. After a couple of easy winters, the trout can be big, but following a tough, cold winter, only a few holdovers survive.

This is a special-regulations lake, with barbless hooks and lures only and a two-trout limit, fourteen inches or larger.

Although there are a few spots where anglers can cast from the shore, float tubes are by far the best way to go. These goldens, like most high-mountain trout, aren't particularly picky about what they'll take, so just about any of the standard nymph or dry patterns will do the job.

McLEOD LAKE AND THE LAKES BASIN

McLeod Lake is one of a series of lakes in the Lakes Basin area just outside the town of Mammoth Lakes, but is the only one with special regulations – strictly catch-and-release, and limited to barbless flies and lures. The others – Mamie, George, Horseshoe, Mary, and Twin Lakes – are stocked, drive-up lakes pounded by all types of anglers. There are a couple of other easy walk-in lakes – Crystal and T.J. – that also offer stocked trout, but get less pressure from anglers.

That said, the Lahontan cutthroats in McLeod aren't that big, usually in the eight-to-twelve-inch range, unless there have been a couple of easy winters that allowed a large population of holdovers. It is less than a mile walk to the lake on a good trail. To get there, take Old Mammoth Road in Mammoth Lakes and follow it southwest to Horseshoe Lake, where the trailhead to McLeod is located. Anglers can fish from the shore, but a float tube offers a better chance to get a multifish day.

Here's a rundown on the lakes in this area.

Twin Lakes: Although usually called Upper Twin and Lower Twin, in fact they share the same water, with a connector stream between. Lower Twin is shallow and has a good deal of weed growth, making it preferred by fly-line types who want to float tube.

Lake Mary: Shoreline access makes it popular with everybody. You can do better elsewhere.

Lake George: Although scenic, it also is deep, making it tough going for fly fishing. The fish are there, but you have to go after them when they are near the surface, usually in the morning or evening. Lake George also is the jumping-off point to get to Crystal and T.J. Lakes, which have a plentiful supply of brookies. The walk to both lakes from George is fairly easy going, and there is shoreline access.

Lake Mamie: This small, shallow lake has heavy weed growth in the summer, making it a good target for float tubing fly fishers.

Horseshoe Lake: The most distant of the easily reached lakes, hence the least fished. It holds rainbows, brookies, and cutthroats.

COTTONWOOD LAKES

The only other special-regulation lakes in this area are much farther south along the eastern slope of the Sierra Nevada and require a 5-mile hike. They are Cottonwood Lakes 1 through 4, part of a six-lake chain near Mount Whitney. They are open July 1 through October 31, with regulations that require artificial lures and flies, barbless hooks, and a zero-take limit.

To get there, take Whitney Portal Road from the town of Lone Pine on Highway 395, then take the road to Horseshoe Meadows Pack Station, where the trailhead is located. The lakes are used to keep brood stock for golden trout and have been open to fishing for only a few years.

Resources

Fly shops in Mammoth Lakes include:

■ **The Trout Fitter**, Shell Mart Center, Highway 203 and Old Mammoth Road, Mammoth Lakes, CA 93546, telephone (760) 924-3676, web site: www.thetroutfitter.com.

■ **The Trout Fly**, Gateway Center, Mammoth Lakes, CA 93546, telephone (760) 934-2157, web site: www.thetroutfly.com, e-mail: troutinfo@aol.com.

■ **Kittredge Sports**, Highway 203 and Forest Trail, Mammoth Lakes, CA 93546, telephone (760) 934-7566.

■ **Rick's Sports Center**, Highway 203 and Center Street, Mammoth Lakes, CA 93546, telephone (760) 934-3416.

The only full-service fly shop in Bishop is **Brock's Flyfishing Specialists**, 100 North Main Street, Bishop, CA 93514, telephone (760) 872-3581.

For information on lodging, camping, restaurants, and so on, contact the **Mammoth Lakes Visitors Bureau**, P.O. Box 48, Mammoth Lakes, CA 93546, telephone (888) 466-2666, web site: www.visitmammoth.com. The e-mail address is mmthvisit@qnet.com.

In the Bishop area, contact the **Bishop Area Chamber of Commerce and Visitor's Bureau**, 690 North Main Street, Bishop, CA 93514, (760) 873-8405, fax (760) 873-6999. Their web site is www.bishopvisitor.com, and the e-mail address is info@bishopvisitor.com.

Woolly Buggers come in all colors and sizes and are probably the most used fly on stillwaters.

Chapter 18

One for the road:
Indian Valley Reservoir

When the nights are long, the weather cold and rainy, and you're suffering from cabin fever, here's a place you can wet a line with little company and lots of room.

Plenty of anglers fish Indian Valley Reservoir, not far from Clear Lake, but most of them come in the summer, and not very many of them are fly fishers. This 7-mile-long reservoir has become known as a kokanee hotspot, but it also holds more than its share of trout. They are stockers, including Eagle Lake strain fish, but they also have plenty of food, and the lake is big enough to support numerous holdovers. It covers 3,800 surface acres when full and is 1,476 feet above sea level.

To get there, take Highway 20, which turns west off Interstate 5 at Williams. Then, 24 miles west of Williams, go north on Walker Ridge Road, which turns off Highway 20. After 6 miles, the road splits, with the right fork going to the upper (northern) end of the reservoir and the left going 4 miles to the southern end, where there is a store, campground, and launch ramp that are open all year. For reasons I don't understand,

A much-used nymph imitation, the Bird's Nest can be tied with or without a beadhead.

The upper end of Indian Valley Reservoir is marked with numerous tree stumps, great hangouts for trout.

the gravel road to the lake has a bad reputation, perhaps because it is dusty in the summer, when most people visit Indian Valley. It is washboardy enough to make your teeth rattle, but otherwise fine – you just have to go slowly in spots.

For fly-line anglers, the best fishing is at the northern end of the lake, where Cache Creek runs in to provide most of the reservoir water. If you have a boat, it probably is easier to put in at the southern end, even though there is a launch fee. If all you have is a float tube, then you'll have to drive to where you want to fish.

Walker Ridge Road, the right fork at the split, will take you to the northern end, where there are several campgrounds and a no-fee boat ramp. It's a tougher drive, and the road can be closed in winter because of storms, but it will put you where the fly fishing is best.

An alternative if you are coming from the west (Highway 101, then Highway 20 east just north of Ukiah) is to take Bartlett Springs Road, which turns north off Highway 20 about a mile east of the town of Nice. It is a winding, 22-mile road, but it takes you to the northern end of Indian Valley Reservoir.

The northern section of the reservoir abounds with the skeletons of trees covered when the reservoir was filled, their barren limbs sticking high above the water when the level drops late in the year. These spots offer protection for all types of fish, including bass, kokanee, and trout. When the water is high, many of these trees are just under the surface, so boaters should go slowly – the reservoir has a 10-mile-per-hour speed limit – and keep a lookout.

A good spot for fly fishers is the Cache Creek arm in the northwestern corner. The road crosses the creek, and it is easy to park and walk to where you can put in with a float tube.

In recent years, the kokanee (a form of landlocked salmon) have come on strong, earning Indian Valley a well-deserved reputation as one of the best kokanee spots in the state. Unfortunately for the fly-line angler, the biggest of the kokanee – up to twenty inches – tend to hold deep in the southern end of the reservoir most of the year.

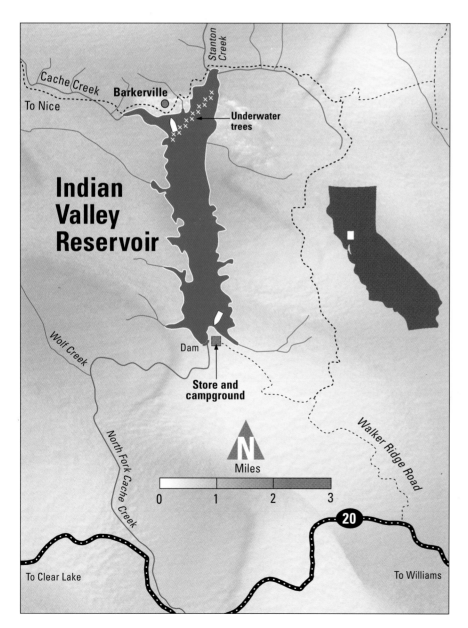

However, in the winter, they'll be found in more shallow areas and for the most part will take the same flies as trout.

Anglers should use the same imitations here as in most other lakes, with the emphasis on big, ugly stuff like Woolly Buggers and Woolly Worms. These are not sophisticated trout that pick and choose what they want to take – you just need to get their attention. Fly-line types can even get away with fishing size 12 and 14 midge imitations throughout the winter months, even though the naturals are several sizes smaller.

Indian Valley is not a pretty reservoir. It is surrounded by sagebrush-covered hills and scrub trees, but you're not there for the scenery. However, there is one bonus during the winter: This is a nesting area for bald and golden eagles.

Eagle Lake rainbows are stocked in Indian Valley Reservoir. Many hold over to become large trout.

Resources

There are no fly shops in the area, so get what you need before you go.

The Clear Lake area, and specifically the town of Clearlake Oaks, is the nearest spot for lodging and restaurants. The **Lake County Marketing Program** has brochures and other information and can be reached at (800) 525-3743. Their address is 875 Lakeport Boulevard, Lakeport, CA 95453, their web site is www.lakecounty.com; e-mail is info@lakecounty.com.

The **Indian Valley Store** at the southern end of the lake has basics, but its fishing gear is aimed at its clientele, bait-and-lure anglers. The store does not have a public telephone, but the folks who run it are very helpful with information once you are there. They have campsites and hookups, in addition to a launch ramp. There also are many other campsites in the vicinity of the lake.

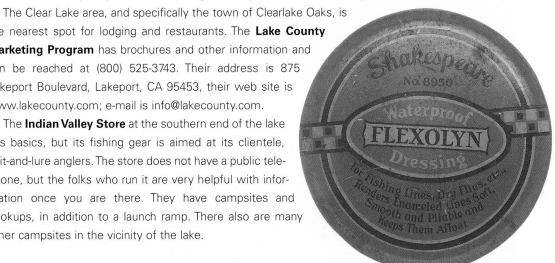

Index

Damselfly nymph imitations are a crucial stillwater fly.

Jay Fair and his German shorthair pointer, Annie, on Eagle Lake.